The Story of the Rosary

THE STORY
OF THE ROSARY

BY

ANNE VAIL

Fount
An Imprint of HarperCollins*Publishers*

Fount Paperbacks is an Imprint of
HarperCollins*Religious*
Part of HarperCollins*Publishers*
77–85 Fulham Palace Road, London W6 8JB

First published in Great Britain
in 1995 by Fount Paperbacks

1 3 5 7 9 10 8 6 4 2

A catalogue record for this book is
available from the British Library

ISBN 0 00 627911-2

Typeset by Harper Phototypesetters Limited
Northampton, England
Printed and bound in Great Britain by
HarperCollinsManufacturing Glasgow

For Dominic, Joanna and Tom
and their families

I would like to thank Father John Buckley SPS for his
advice and encouragement, and John Vail without
whose reassuring support this book would not
have been written.

INTRODUCTION

This book is the result of a recent experience in Italy, which began a long search into the history of the rosary.

My journey took me through Tuscany, through countryside little changed since the painters of the Renaissance described the small hill-top villages with their guardian cypress trees, and hills covered with vineyards. Even the domes and towers of Florence emerging through the mist that settles over the river Arno looked wonderfully familiar.

I reached Florence in late September, and the heat of late summer hung over the city. Mornings were spent exploring labyrinthine streets, past palaces and monasteries and through crowded markets that thrive in the smallest corners imaginable, and then over the Ponte Vecchio which bears a row of shops across the Arno with such charm.

In the Piazza della Signoria crowds listened to the guides recounting the drama of the bonfire of the vanities, when the Dominican Savonarola turned his wrath and disapproval on the luxury of the Medicis and burnt all their books. Years later, unable to contain his rage, he turned his fury on the Borgias and paid with his life in that same square.

A short journey from the city centre and one enters another world in the monastery of San Marco. Although the stern figure of Savanarola still broods in the shadows of the church beside the monastery, within the dormitory of San Marco are the paintings of Fra Angelico, and one is immediately aware of a deeper and more spiritual wonder that was Renaissance Florence.

Through all these images there is the inescapable jostling of the crowds, visitors anxiously holding guide books and camera in a balancing act that permits only the briefest glance at anything, the people of Florence eagerly capitalizing on this endless procession, and over all this there is the stupefying heat that engulfs the city.

By mid-afternoon, those in the know have vanished to siesta in the cool, shaded by the endless pots of geraniums that clutter the smallest of verandahs. Although the newcomer is momentarily startled at his good luck at finding the city empty, it is only shortlived for soon the shops will lift their shutters, the churches will open and Florence will be awake again.

In an attempt to find shade, I leant on a small wooden door and found myself in the Church of the Annunciation, momentarily blinded by the darkness and shocked at the echoing stillness as the roar of the traffic was silenced by the door swinging closed behind me. Gradually my eyes grew accustomed to the gloom, and through the stone arches I was able to see kneeling figures, beads in hand, casting long shadows on the wall beyond.

In the suffused light, I could see above the figures a panel displaying a pillar of roses with the words "Rosa Mystica" written in clear relief below.

There were only a dozen or so women, clad in black, and in the cool air time seemed suspended, revealing a scene from a bygone age, long since forgotten or overlooked by the world that rushed past beyond the cloisters.

The sight before me was so familiar that it scarcely registered on my preoccupied mind, and yet something caused me to stop, and with a growing awareness, I realized that months, perhaps years, had passed since I had last heard that familiar prayer, a soft murmuring without inflection. Somehow I had presumed that while time fled past, somewhere those devout souls were fingering their beads, and in their rhythmic devotion lay the promise of sanity in a confused world.

I was aware of the apparitions at Lourdes and Fatima, and more recently of the accounts of appearances of the Virgin Mary in countries of Eastern Europe and Spain. There appeared to be the same message for penance and prayer, specifically the prayer of the rosary, for peace in the world. 'I am the lady of the rosary' Mary said to the children at Fatima, and the urgency of the message has increased as the twentieth century approaches the millennium.

While many people have listened to her profound words, for others the prayer of the rosary is an anachronism, and more and more bizarre means have been sought in the search for a panacea for the turbulence and confusion of life today.

Not long ago I was listening to a radio lecture given by an eminent psychiatrist to an audience whose members were searching for a means of finding peace and sanity in the stressful lives that they led.

His method involved the total relaxation of the body, followed by the gentle repetition of a mantra or form of words, and finally the focusing of the mind on a subject worthy of infinite reflection. By mastering this technique, he suggested, one could find the peace of mind to cope with the stress of modern life. Absentmindedly I thought 'Yes. We were taught that by the nuns when we were children, and it is called the rosary.'

Although it is considered to be merely repetitious by many, the rosary is going through an astonishing transition and it is difficult to think of a prayer that is more perfectly in tune with the needs of today.

As I sat in the shadows of the Church of the Annunciation, listening to those women at prayer, I thought again of the paintings of Fra Angelico, and of the object of his prayer and devotion. For he was describing an inner world, a more personal world in which his entire being was concentrated on the mystery of God's love for mankind. His frescoes are a visual prayer exploring the ultimate love of God made man, the story of the Incarnation that is the prayer of the rosary.

The devotion of those elderly women for their rosaries can be mystifying to those who have no knowledge of its history, and yet those same women would probably be unaware that such a story existed and would find any explanation quite unnecessary.

But the cloistered other-worldliness of such a gathering illustrates an exclusivity that is misleading, and this book is an attempt to open the windows and to bring the rosary into the daylight.

As a means of counting, beads have been used since the earliest times, from the abacus, still in use in some parts of the world, to the familiar worry beads of Eastern religions. In areas of great danger, soldiers will silently count their footsteps on beads made from knotted string, to enable them to concentrate on every sound that assails them.

In the same practical way, rosary beads have accompanied kings and statesmen, monks and nuns, and ordinary men and women who have found comfort in the touch of a bead, the prayer it counts, and the sense of proportion in life offered by the contemplation of the scriptures which makes up the prayer of the rosary.

The beginning of the story of the rosary describes a vanished world, a world more in tune with the elements and seasons, when a man reaped what he sowed and the parallel with his spiritual life was one that he understood and accepted.

The second chapter deals with the formation of the prayer and in particular its origins in England, in the prayer of saints and soldiers, of John of Gaunt and Thomas à Becket. It shows how the customs of that time, the constant movement of pilgrims to one shrine or another, the general air of festivity on the feast days of the saints and of Mary especially, made the rosary a particularly English affair.

My search took me far beyond England, and I travelled to Albi in France, to Venice and to great houses whose owners are the custodians of historic rosaries. Because this was above all a spiritual journey, I travelled to Fatima and Lourdes.

In Fatima I joined the thousands of pilgrims in a procession that wound its way past the place where Our Lady appeared in 1917, and where the prayer of the rosary is recited in every language throughout the day and night. The atmosphere is one of great urgency in the longing for peace in the world, and at the same time one of immense hope. But the first discovery, and the source of all that followed, was the importance of gardens and gardening in the life of prayer of the early Christian. It is therefore with gardens that the story of the rosary begins.

Chapter One

The story told by the rosary
Is the story of primitive beauty,
True as the burden of folk-songs
It is a song piped on the hills
By a shepherd calling his sheep.

From *The Rosary* by Caryll Houselander

✛

The word rosary has two meanings and at first glance there seems little connection between them.

Until the twelfth century any Englishman would have staked, if not his life, at least his hat, on the knowledge that a rosary or roserie was an enclosed garden for roses. Even today some horticulturalists will insist that a roserie is the correct term for such an area, in the same way that they would describe an arboretum for trees.

The mere suggestion of roses and enclosed gardens conveys an air of mystery and delight, for the rose is the acknowledged favourite of the flower garden and conjures up images of secret gardens, of Alice In Wonderland stumbling into the giant rose garden. And for the English there is the knowledge that the rose had for centuries been the emblem of their country, long before the Tudors adopted the rose for their own.

During the latter part of the twelfth century a different meaning to the word rosary came into the language. A small circlet of beads carried by clergy and laity alike, bearing no similarity to a rose, was given the name by country people, gradually becoming universal in that strange way customs have. And then a Dominican monk named Thomas de Cintempre formally acknowledged this title by a chance remark in the thirteenth century.

The Oxford Dictionary defines a rosary as a rose garden and as a form of devotion in which five or fifteen decades of

Aves are repeated, each decade preceded by a Paternoster, and followed by the Gloria. For the sake of definition this is a neat distinction, but as the panel of roses in the Church of the Annunciation in Florence hinted, the rose as a symbol is a vital part of the rosary. The two images overlap like a tapestry whose different threads, meaningless on their own, gradually come together to form a picture.

There can be a few words that cast a more vivid impression of the importance of gardens to the early Christians than the words of Genesis: 'And the Lord God had planted a paradise of pleasure from the beginning; wherein He placed man whom He had formed.'[1]

Whatever may be revealed in later centuries in the search for the history of the rosary, those few words explain that the connection with gardens was no romantic whim but one placed firmly in biblical allusion.

So much has been written about Paradise and yet we are as far as ever from any precise understanding of its nature, and however time and custom bring subtle changes to our language, the word remains unaltered in its meaning. For all that, we are surprisingly vague about the precise nature of the vision that it brings to mind.

The actual site of the Garden of Eden occupied the imagination of numerous scholars and hopeful travellers throughout the early centuries as they searched in vain for an earthly Paradise. On some medieval maps, the Garden is shown on the plains bordering the great Euphrates river, not far from the spot on which Nebuchadnezzar planted the Hanging Gardens of Babylon for his homesick bride from the mountains.

In the fourteenth century Sir John Mandeville confidently explained to his bemused readers that the Garden of Eden was perched on a mountain of such immense height that as it moved through the sky, the moon touched its lawns.

Although there were undoubtedly differing opinions as to

the existence of the Garden of Eden, either in a material or spiritual form, it was the latter which became the accepted view of the Christian Church. To the writers of the Old Testament, however, the existence of Paradise was beyond question in both senses.

From the practical point of view, the ideal garden figures as the earliest home of the human race. A place for the souls of the blessed in the traditions of nearly all the ancient nations.

From the moment of banishment from Paradise, the arrival of the new Eve who would bring forth the Messiah was anticipated, both in the writings of the Old Testament and by an exiled people labouring under a sense of loss, for the union of the Creator with His created is the sublime and at the same time the most natural state of affairs. Those early writers seem unerringly to increase the sense of loss in the emphasis placed on the very things that were painfully absent from the lives of the exiles. The different elements of the Paradise Garden were dwelt on and repeated with tantalizing frequency, and references to the new Eve were couched in terms that were only too readily understood.

In the accounts of Genesis, the Tree of Knowledge dominates all else, creating at the same time the second element of shade and with it the suggestion of peace and respite from the relentless heat.

The third and equally important element of the Paradise Garden was water. In a terrain of such wilderness, where little or no rain fell for six months of the year, the gardens of Palestine, like those of Egypt and Persia, were a network of elaborately arranged waterways.

Isaiah uses the imagery of a watered garden to great effect: 'and the Lord will give thee rest continually and will fill thy soul with brightness and deliver thy bones; and thou shalt be like a watered garden and like a fountain of water whose waters shall not fail.'[2] To the people of Egypt, few words could have been more eloquent. Water was looked upon as a treasure beyond compare and a source of life, and in biblical writings it is always seen as the symbol of the Holy Spirit.

In the Song of Solomon the truly spiritual nature of the Old Testament is most vividly portrayed, for the Song speaks of the Virgin Mary and the garden is the symbol of the Beloved of Christ, with apt allusion to the treasure of water. 'My sister, my spouse is a garden enclosed, a fountain sealed up.'[3] In poetic terms, an exiled people learnt of the promise of the new Eve and the Christ Child who would lead man back to Paradise, and in the allusive language of the Old Testament writers, the new Eve was compared to a garden enclosing heaven and earth.

The image of the enclosed garden could hardly have been more evocative to the early Christian, and the effect of the description of Mary as the '*hortens conclusus*' was one in which complex mysteries were unravelled with enviable simplicity. The subject was taken up by painters of the Middle Ages, who with exquisite care illustrated this profound mystery for people who were often unable to read or write but were accustomed, by means of intricate symbols, to 'read' the picture placed before them.

The words of the Song 'Like a fountain enclosed' were an inspiration to painters, and these pictures were brimming with allegory and meaning. In the '*Virgin of the Fountain*' painted by Jan van Eyck in the fifteenth century, Our Lady is portrayed with the Infant beside the symbolic fountain, and as if to underline the message it carries, the Child trails a rosary on one small finger.

There were biblical clues to the choice of the rose itself as an emblem of Our Lady. 'Like a rose planted on the rivers I have borne fruit' are the words taken from Ecclesiasticus, and from the Song of Songs come the words 'I am the rose of Sharon, the lily of the valleys.'

The 'Rose of the Virgin' and the 'Rose Mariae' are the names given to the rose of Jericho, a small plant native to the deserts of Arabia, and there is a legend that this rose sprang from the earth beneath the feet of the Holy Family as they fled into Egypt.

And so the rose left its place in mythology and was chosen naturally as if this had always been its role, reaching its height in the celestial rose of Dante in the fourteenth century.

To Dante, no other flower was of sufficient beauty to express the mystery of the Incarnation. Only the rose could symbolize the miracle of Divine love brought down to earth, and to him the Blessed Virgin was the 'rose wherein the word Divine was made Incarnate.'[4]

In the 'Virgin of the Rose Garden' by Stefano da Zevio, Mary is seated with the Holy Child on her lap beside a sparkling fountain. The Garden is enclosed by an exotic trellis of roses with birds and angels perched precariously amongst the leaves, and in the foreground St Catherine is weaving a garland of roses.

As the onlooker gazes with his thoughts on the mother peacefully showing us her Child, we seem included in that air of intimacy, for she looks serenely beyond the Child. Although the scene appears to be intensely private, it is somehow not exclusive and we are enveloped in her glance, as if her happiness were not complete without our accord.

In many paintings the chaplet of roses forms the enclosure, almost as if the roses themselves had taken root to grow into towering hedges. Although it is tempting and convenient to draw conclusions from the work of artists, the repeated choice of this subject does imply that the idea was popular and readily understood.

As if to underline this acceptance, there is an instruction attached to the painting of 'Mary, the Enclosed Garden' which tells the artist that the perimeter or enclosure need only be indicated with a garland or chaplet of roses.

Although those simple words of advice from an unknown patron to an equally unknown artist seem at first glance to be of little importance, as a clue in the search for the origin of the name of Our Lady's prayer, they are revealing. For those words imply, however casually, that the chaplet or garland of roses had joined that precious vocabulary of readily understood images.

'Let us crown ourselves with rose-buds' says the book of Wisdom, and in the Middle Ages garlands became a sign of heavenly joy. For the garland or circle was not only decorative but a constant reminder of the 'enclosed garden' foreshadowing the circle of beads which would gather men's thoughts to the mystery of the Incarnation.

In England Whit Sunday was often known as Rose Sunday, and with garlands made from the briar rose of the hedgerows, known by children as 'Sweet Maria', processions wound their way down the lanes of every village in the month of May, which is traditionally the month of Mary.

Centuries later, when the word 'garland' or 'chaplet' became used as the name of our Lady's beads, some of the Church authorities were to object strongly on the grounds that it was worldly, insisting that the title 'Our Lady's Psalter' be used. But the garland of roses had become a sign of the circle of beads enclosing the mystery of the Incarnation, and even today the title given to rosary beads in German is '*rosenkranz*', crown of roses.

The word 'rosary' could perhaps have remained as the title given to garlands or chaplets of roses, replete with heavenly connections, used either as coronets or to decorate altars and candles, always in honour of the Blessed Virgin.

However, things did not rest there. In the eleventh and twelfth centuries collections of prayers in honour of Mary were being written under such titles as 'The Garden of Roses' or simply 'Rosarium', not in the cloying way of romantic novelists, but with monastic understanding of the similarity of the

8

work of a gardener and the Christian life of prayer.

Gradually, the roses had become prayers whose tally was kept by means of beads, and the prayers are there for the sake of the mysteries of the New Testament which make up the meditations of the rosary. For the biblical references to gardens are not restricted to the Old Testament. The three most important events of the New Testament take place in gardens: the Agony in the Garden, the Crucifixion and the Resurrection.

Fra Angelico's masterpiece, 'Noli me tangere', portrays the risen Christ in an enclosed garden of rare beauty, in which delicate flowers and leaves increase the notion of Paradise, underlining with gentle simplicity the implication of the Resurrection. In this picture, as in many others, the Redeemer is portrayed with spade in hand, to show that His work was complete.

The message that prayer and sacrifice must precede salvation, so vividly illustrated by these events, was not missed by the early desert monks. These holy men were the first to understand not merely the symbolic importance of a garden, but in a more practical sense they compared the toil of cultivating a garden with that of a life of prayer, and through both the will of God was made known to them.

When St Anthony the Great took to the desert in the third century he cultivated and pruned a little garden, not only to provide herbs for himself but also for the nourishment of his visitors after their arduous journey. On one occasion an angel appeared to him and proceeded to plait a mat with the palm leaves, and then paused to pray before resuming work with the words: 'Do thus, and thou shalt be saved.'[5] In this way the link between work and prayer was emphasized, and so was forged the connection between gardens and prayer that led eventually to the prayer of the rosary itself.

So deeply did the early hermits understand that the loving care and labour of tending a garden was a direct parallel to prayer that another desert monk, St Phocan, remains to this day the patron saint of gardeners.

St Phocan dwelt outside the gate of Sinope and lived, the story of his life states quite simply, by cultivating a garden. Under Diocletian, orders were sent out for his arrest and soldiers were despatched to find him. Having lost their way, the men stopped unwittingly at the home of the saint, who, moved by pity, took them in and cared for them. Under the warmth of his kindness, they explained their task, whereupon the saint promised to reward their search the following day. After his guests had retired to bed, St Phocan went into the garden and in prayer he prepared his grave. In the morning he led the soldiers into the garden explaining his identity and there, amongst his flowers, he died.

From these early beginnings, the importance of gardening in Christian monasticism was firmly established, and further endorsed by St Benedict in his Rule, which laid down strict instruction on the form and cultivation of the monastery garden. There is in existence a plan of the ideal Benedictine monastery which was drawn up for the Abbot of St Gall in Switzerland in the middle of the ninth century. The plan shows three gardens, one of medicinal herbs which are listed in great detail, the kitchen garden and thirdly the orchard with fruit trees planted in straight lines so that the graves of the monks could be laid between them.[6]

In later centuries roses were planted in the monks' cemetery in anticipation of Paradise and of the Blessed Virgin who awaited them in heaven.[7]

Cardinal Newman has described the Benedictines as the custodians of civilization throughout the Dark Ages, for while danger and chaos held sway elsewhere, within the monastery walls, the monks continued their life of prayer and work, as instructed by the Rule laid down in the sixth century. They became a lifeline to the community, not only in the spiritual sense, but also for their teaching and farming expertise.

Benedictine land was farmed for grain and the traditional water fountain of the early Paradise gardens was translated into large fish ponds seething with carp for the refectory table. Amongst the fruit orchards beyond the vineyards stood the beehives, and beyond that lay the herb gardens.

In 840, Walafrid Strabo, a Benedictine monk, wrote a poem entitled 'The Little Garden' which relates in some detail the plants that were grown at the time of Charlemagne. Although written over a thousand years ago, it presents a vivid picture of the old monk toiling over his garden as he struggled with the nettles whose roots were like 'basket-work'. The discouragement is only fleeting, for he quickly passes on to describe his favourite plants, the lily and the rose.

The Carthusians, however, lived in cells constructed in such a manner that no view of other humans was possible, and each cell led into a private garden in which the inhabitant grew herbs to sustain his frugal existence.

In the solid uncompromising stone remains of Mount Grace Priory in Yorkshire, where no concession was made to beauty, the silent ruins bear witness to a life of stark simplicity where no diversion could be allowed, and the gardens, once loved and laboured over, lie abandoned to a riot of weeds. And yet occasionally the eye is caught by wild flowers flourishing amongst the chaos, proclaiming that all is never lost.

To those intrepid monks, their gardens were not seen as a diversion but as an echo of Paradise to which all must aspire. Even so not everyone was capable of such perfection, and there must have been occasions when the love of gardening and pride in his own industry tempted the lonely monk to peer over the wall at his neighbour's work, or even to succumb to a moment of earthly pride in the results of his labours. Some indeed became so enthralled by their gardens that a writer named Heffad of Landsberg, in a work entitled *Hortus Deliciarum*, related the sad fate of a monk who had climbed to the top of the ladder of holiness only to glance down at his garden, thereby losing his balance and falling to the ground, forfeiting all for the love of his earthly paradise.

In less enclosed orders, paradise gardens were created and placed symbolically near the entrance to the abbey church. This was in part an influence of the early eastern gardens, for glowing accounts of Persian gardens were sent home by the Ambassadors to the courts of the Caliphs of Baghdad, describing lawns usually divided by paths with a central fountain, inhabited by peacocks and exotic birds. These gardens were aptly named paradise gardens.

Bishop Etholwold of Winchester (908-984) built an abbey at Thorne later described by William of Malmesbury as being set in a paradise. The paradise garden in this case was the domain of the sacristan, in which he grew flowers, mainly roses and lilies, for the decoration of the church.

In addition to the altars, shrines and statues of the saints and even the candles were encircled with flowers. Sometimes the symbolism was not restricted to the flower of the rose alone but the whole bush or tree was used to illustrate the undoubted labour required to achieve sanctity.

In an engraving of the sixteenth century, three Dominican monks – Joseph Sprenger, Alanus du Rupe and St Dominic himself – are to be seen tending a rose tree within an enclosed garden above which Our Lady extends in her hand a circle of rosary beads.

The theme of the rose tree is used again in the *Secret of the Rosary* written in the seventeenth century by St Louis de Montfort. The book opens with the author's dedication offered in the form of roses, thus a white rose for priests, a red rose for sinners and a mystical rose tree for devout souls. This last dedication he elaborates thus:

'Its green leaves are the joyful mysteries, the thorns the sorrowful ones, and the flowers the glorious mysteries . . . eventually this little seed will grow so great that the birds of heaven will dwell in it and make their nests there. Its shade will shelter them from the scorching heat of the sun and its great height will keep them safe from the wild beasts on the ground.'

He concludes the dedications with a rosebud for children. The body of the book is divided into fifty small sections reflecting the number of Aves in the Psalter, each one entitled numerically as a rose, and it remains the most authoritative work on the subject of the rosary.

This preoccupation with plants and prayer was not in the least sentimental. In most cases the monks existed on the produce they eked from the soil, and the rigours of their lives left little room for day-dreaming, nor did they show any inclination to do to. It was rather a recognition of the humble role of the gardener, of the fleeting glimpse of mortality enshrined in the earth to which all must return, and above all the lesson to be learnt from the quiet attendance on the will of God.

✧

CHAPTER TWO

Ring a ring of roses
A pocket full of posies
Atishoo atishoo
We all fall down

Anon.

When the Dark Ages drew to a close in the eleventh century, a period of peace and relative prosperity followed, and gardening became a popular pastime. Under the Normans, English gardens became the subject of renewed attention, and as many of the Norman lords had returned to England from conquering southern Italy and Moorish Spain, the influence of the eastern Garden of Paradise became apparent. Strolling amongst the scented flowers and lawns must have induced an air of thoughtful contemplation wholly unknown until then, and not surprisingly Mary is acknowledged in the naming of the flowers, for the devotion to the Virgin that had steadily grown over the preceding centuries now grew on a wave of enthusiasm.

The snowdrop was known as 'Our Lady of February', lungwort as 'Our Lady's milk-worte' from the Annunciation, marigolds belonged to all her feasts, and it was well known that the lily bloomed from the Visitation to St Swithun's.

It is difficult today to understand fully the depth of affection for the Virgin Mary and the saints amongst men and women of the Middle Ages, for they were seen as sympathetic intermediaries between the people and their Lord. They looked on the saints as their amiable companions and friends, people to whom they turned constantly for help and support in all the vicissitudes of their lives, as they would to dear and trusted friends. Over and above all the saints, Mary, as the mother of their Saviour, was the patroness *par excellence*, and England was the acknowledged dower of the Virgin.

Until recently there was a picture in the English College in Rome which shows King Richard II and his Queen, assisted by St John the Baptist, offering the map of England to the Virgin while she smiles her acceptance, so that although we have no precise date of the naming of Our Lady's dower, we know that the idea was familiar enough in the fourteenth century. There are few traces left today of this Marian tradition, although probably more than can at first be recognized. Some places still bear lingering witness, such as Ottery St Mary or St Mary Clyst in Devon, St Mary Bourne in Hampshire, and in London, the familiar Marylebone which comes from Mary la Bonne, and there are others too numerous to mention.

But these are merely ghostly signposts in a country where once the chapels and shrines were a constant reminder of the affection in which Mary was held, a country in which St George could be described by his biographer as 'Our Lady's Knight', for he was and is still the patron of her dowry. Even the title 'Our Lady' appears to have been used first in England.

In 'Our Lady's Dowry' Father Bridgett quotes a witness at the canonization of St Thomas of Cantalupe, Bishop of Hereford in 1330, who invoked 'Our Lady'.[1] The Italian Commissioner enquired which lady she meant, and she replied that of course she meant the Lady of Heaven.

The custom of venerating Mary in this country stretches back to the fifth century and can be dated from the introduction of Christianity. The first Christian church in England was built at Glastonbury and was described by William of Malmesbury as a 'holy and ancient spot, chosen and sanctified by God, in honour of the Immaculate Virgin Mary, Mother of God.'[2]

In pre-Reformation days, England had sixteen hundred

churches dedicated to the patronage of the Virgin, not to mention countless religious houses, colleges and shrines. This may seem an astonishing number and adds fuel to the frequent misunderstanding of Marian devotion, which can appear to be somewhat out of balance, and thus obscures the importance placed on it by Christian theologians. There is a clear distinction to be drawn for it is, in effect, devotion through Mary. Christian teaching has always maintained that as the Mother of God, her life was spent in honour of her Son, and that man should honour the Blessed Virgin by following her example. From the time of St Augustine, churches have been built in honour of Mary in England, and poems and prayers written in praise of the role of the Blessed Virgin as mediatrix with her Son.

Writing in the twelfth century, the learned Cistercian Abbot, Aelred of Rievaulx, whose chronicles follow the tradition laid down by earlier monks, expressed this complex teaching to his followers thus:

'The greatness of Mary's love for men is proved by the many miracles and many visions by which the Lord deigns to show that she especially intercedes with her Son for the whole human race. It is vain for me to even attempt to show how great is her charity; no human mind is able to even attempt to show how great is her charity; no human mind is able to conceive it.'[3]

Throughout the Dark Ages, from the days of the Roman Empire until the millennium, the turbulent nature of the time meant that for most people life was full of suffering. Hardship and disaster were their constant companions as plagues and wars overtook them with little or no warning, and through all these calamities it seemed as though Mary would be their refuge and strength in an age of great paternalism and also of great cruelty.

The Venerable Bede alone seems to shine like a beacon in the wilderness of those times, writing from the draughty abbey of Jarrow in the eighth century, and his many texts and sermons bear witness to his devotion to the Blessed Virgin.

At first he seemed intent on proving the holiness of the Blessed Virgin and, having proved that beyond doubt, he turned to dwell upon her joys. This link with the mysteries of the rosary and also the convenience of his name have frequently earned for him the authorship of the rosary. Although this was not so, the theory would undoubtedly have appealed to that holy man.

The Venerable Bede died in 735, and in the year of his death another great Benedictine, Alcuin, was born, a man who was to spend many years of his life in York before going for a time to the court of Charlemagne. He too was a great devotee of Mary, and on one occasion he sent home a description of his monastic cell in Tours which he had decorated with white lilies and red roses in her honour.

Before he travelled to France in 780, whilst Charlemagne was setting out to do battle with the Saracens and the cries of Roland were echoing around the Valley of Roncevalles, Alcuin composed his mass in honour of the Virgin Mary, known as the Mary Mass. Although, as St Augustine points out, mass can be offered to God alone, the Mary Mass is one in which the Blessed Virgin is especially commemorated.

The Mary Mass became popular and there were numerous occasions when bequests were made to support the Saint Mary priest, as he was called, and in many houses the Mary Mass was celebrated every day in a private chapel. As dawn broke, the bell known as the Mary Bell, rang to awaken everyone and announce the hour of prayer.

In the *Valor Ecclesiasticus* there is mention of a sum of money paid to the clerics and choristers who sang the Mass of the Blessed Virgin in Salisbury Cathedral each day, and in 1215 land was given by the Bishop of St Paul's in London to the poor clerks of the choir who sang the office of Our Lady after the Mary Mass.

The early mass on Our Lady's feast was known as the glutton mass, for anyone who was out of bed in time to attend was then free to enjoy themselves for the rest of the day.

The feasts of the Virgin Mary were enthusiastically celebrated, and laws were passed to ensure that nothing should stand in the way of the general amusement. In the time of King Alfred, laws were passed to give freemen a week's holiday before the feast of the Assumption on 15 August, and in Walsingham King Henry III granted the right to hold a fair lasting six days before Our Lady's birthday in September.

Some feasts had been celebrated for hundreds of years, indeed when St Augustine led his followers to Canterbury in the sixth century he found that the feast of the Purification of Mary had become part of the calendar under the influence of Roman missionaries of earlier times. The feast of the Immaculate Conception was of particular importance in England, for it was first celebrated in this country, an enterprise which caused heated controversy between the English and French clergy as to the exact date of its origin. The feast was instituted by St Anselm who came to England from the Abbey of Bec at the end of the eleventh century. Psalms were adapted in praise of Mary, especially in England, and anyone who was unable to read or remember the psalms repeated the greeting of the Angel Gabriel at the Annunciation. Both the Venerable Bede and St Aelred, Abbot of Rievaulx, wrote long sermons on the subject of the Annunciation, and the Angelic salutation formed part of their prayer. By the end of the twelfth century, the clergy of Paris were listing the Ave Maria together with the Credo and Paternoster as prayers that the faithful were required to know. In England the same instructions were given by St Richard of Chichester in 1246, and the Bishop of Durham followed suit in 1255.

At that stage, the prayer consisted of the Angelic salutation alone. In the *Reliquae Antiquae* there are many examples of the various forms of the Ave Maria prayer, and there is one which is said to date from a manuscript of the thirteenth century:

'Marie ful off grace, weel de be,
Godd of hevene be with thee,
Oure alle wimmen bliscedd tu be,
So be the bern datt is boren of thee.'

The words of St Elizabeth, 'Blessed is the fruit of thy womb', were soon added, and eventually the words 'Holy Mary, Mother of God, pray for us sinners now and at the hour of our death' completed the prayer.

The last part of the prayer touches on one of the main preoccupations of the Christian in the Middle Ages. It would not be an exaggeration to say that in the midst of life they were not only surrounded by death, but they were frequently overtaken by it without warning. The inevitability of death was ever present, although the dire admonishments of the clergy give a false impression of the mood of the laity.

The constant reminders of impending hell fire meted out from the pulpit, far from revealing a morbidity amongst the people, suggest that on the contrary they often failed to treat it with the solemnity deemed fit by the clergy.

Their feelings merely underline the great trust placed in their special saints, and above all their mediatrix, the Virgin Mary. On many occasions the Blessed Virgin was known to warn those facing an unexpected death, for it was not death itself they feared, but the punishment of Purgatory or worse still, Hell, that awaited those who died ill prepared. They had unshakeable confidence that Mary, their advocate, would be there to plead for them before the courts of Heaven.

There is a wall painting in the Commandery at Worcester dating from these times, which vividly illustrates this trust in

Mary the Advocate. The somewhat primitive picture relates the story of St Michael weighing the souls of the dead. There he stands, the judge of souls, with the scales of justice in one hand and in the other a flaming sword, apparently unaware and unperturbed by whatever the result might be. In one panier is a little soul, just dead, who peers anxiously at the other panier which is weighed down by a large bundle marked 'sins'. To his horror the scale is further drawn down by a large devil. What the little soul cannot see is the figure of the Mother of God, standing behind him. She observes all that is happening, has realized that two can play at that game, and she is dropping her rosary, bead by bead, into the scale of the poor frightened soul, so that to his amazement, his scale is more heavily weighed down.

When the final words of the Hail Mary, 'Pray for us sinners now and at the hour of our death', were added, they were recited therefore with deep confidence born of a conviction that they expressed no less than the proven truth.

These were the prayers the people knew and recited, for themselves and for the souls of their departed friends and families, and in a practical sense to keep pace with the prayer of the monastery.

The total recited usually seems to have been one hundred and fifty, reflecting the number of psalms in the Psalter of St David, on which every monastery of the time based the daily worship. The tally reached almost mythological heights, especially in Ireland, where the influence of St Patrick had further divided the number into three, known as the 'three fifties'. Even in the legend of King Arthur and his Knights of the Round Table, an allegory for man's search for Paradise, the number of his knights was carefully chosen to reflect the number of psalms in the Psalter.

In the eleventh century, the first acknowledged step towards the arrangement of the rosary was taken by St Anselm, then Archbishop of Canterbury. He composed a prayer to Mary which was based on the psalms and consisted of one hundred and fifty verses, which he divided into three, each verse commencing with the word 'ave'.

The prayer, which was written for his monks at Canterbury to recite each day, must have been offered many times for the saint himself as he struggled with the King over the respective rights of the Church and Crown. He named this prayer 'Our Lady's Psalter', the first official prayer of this name, and the legends that sprang up at the time give some idea of the interest that greeted St Anselm's prayer.

One, entitled 'How Our Levidi's Sauter was first Founde', comes from a Scottish manuscript which relates the story of a young man saying his fifty Aves daily. Mary appeared before him meanly dressed, and when he enquired the reason for this, she replied that this was due to the short measure of his prayers, and more were needed.[4]

In the fourteenth century, a famous Carthusian monk, Henry Egher, claimed to have had a remarkable vision of Our Lady in which she taught him how to say the 'Psalter' in her honour. This he described to one of the priors of his Order in England, and within a short space of time the prayer became known throughout the country, with far-reaching effects.

In the same century Eton College was founded by Henry VI in honour of Our Lady, and the original seal of the college depicts the Assumption of the Virgin with the Royal Arms inscribed beneath. The statutes of the College required the students to say each day 'the complete psalter of the Blessed Virgin consisting of a credo, fifteen Paters and one hundred and fifty Ave Marias', and this was in accordance with the instruction given by Our Lady to the Carthusian monk.

The choristers were instructed to recite the hours of Mary each day, and a final practical note required that each scholar should recite the Office of Our Lady whilst making his bed.

Other institutions, including King's College, Cambridge,

received similar instructions, and the choristers were obliged to recite the hours of Mary each day.

Gradually, from being based on the psalms, the ave-psalter began to develop a clear character of its own, and the division into the fifties came to represent the three moods or humours that make up the rosary – the joyful, sorrowful and glorious mysteries. Perhaps this was prompted by the wish to have a prayer that was different from the office of the monasteries, but it was undoubtedly influenced by the working knowledge of the scriptures enjoyed by many.

Much of the popularity of the joys is said to have been due to St Thomas à Becket, who was the Archbishop of Canterbury during the turbulent reign of King Henry II. St Thomas was a hero to his followers, for he defended the rights of the Church with a fervour that was to cost him his life. In quieter moments he composed a hymn on the seven joys of Our Lady, listing the visiting of the Magi, the Finding in the Temple, the Annunciation, the Birth of Christ, the Resurrection, the Ascension and the Assumption. The first two joys were frequently omitted to leave five, although the number did vary, for John of Gaunt left fifteen pieces of silver to the Carmelites in London in honour of fifteen joys.

As if to find some practical way of demonstrating the new interest in the joys of Mary, the custom grew of lighting candles before her statue. Usually five in number to reflect the five wounds of Christ, these candles were frequently decorated with garlands of flowers and known as 'gauds', and later the word was used to describe the large bead that separates the Ave beads from the Paternoster, between the mysteries of the rosary.

The most elaborate arrangements were made to ensure that after the death of the supplicant the candle would continue to burn before Our Lady's statue, and even cattle or sheep were bequeathed to support the cost. The custom was not restricted to country people, for King Henry VIII kept candles burning at the shrines of Our Lady of Doncaster and Our Lady of Walsingham, which were known as King's candles.

A detailed instruction on the recitation of prayers with the five joys of Our Lady is to be found in the *Ancren Riwle*, the rule set down by the Bishop of Salisbury for the nuns of a convent at Tarrent in Dorset. Writing early in the thirteenth century, the Bishop sets out prayers on the joys of Mary, each consisting of a short dissertation commencing with the words 'Sweet Lady, St Mary' and naming in turn the Annunciation, the Birth, the Resurrection, the Ascension and the Coronation of Our Lady in Heaven. After each reading, five Hail Mary's are to be recited and he adds, 'After her five highest joys count in the anthems. Cause to be written on a scroll what ye do not know by heart.'

The Bishop of Salisbury can have little suspected that his gentle rule for those Dorsetshire nuns would continue to be a source of inspiration for hundreds of years to come. Written with a mixture of humility and severity, it is full of the practical means of achieving sanctity and, as is only natural in the rugged country existence of the place and time, he often illustrates his point with down-to-earth simplicity.

On the subject of talkativeness, he is firm: 'Eve in Paradise held a long conversation with the serpent, and told him all the lessons that God had taught her and Adam concerning the apple; thus the fiend by her talk understood, at once, her weakness, and found out the way to ruin her. Our Lady, Saint Mary, acted in quite a different manner. She told the Angel no tale, but asked him briefly that which she wanted to know. Do you, my dear sister, imitate Our Lady and not the cackling of Eve. Wherefore, let an anchoress, whatsoever she be, keep silence as much as ever she can and may. Let her not have the hen's nature; when the hen has laid she must needs to cackle. And what does she get by it? Straightway comes the chough and robs her of her eggs and devours all that of which she should have brought forth the live birds. And just so the wicked chough, the devil . . .'

On the subject of the joys of Mary he instructed them to pray 'Sweet Lady, Saint Mary, receive my salutation with the same 'Ave' and make me to think little of every outward delight, and comfort me within, and by thy merits procure for me the joy of heaven.' He concludes his rule with the words 'As often as ye read anything in this book greet the Lady with an Ave Maria and for him who made this rule, and for him who wrote it and took pains about it. Moderate enough I am, who asks so little', and one can only imagine that they must have been happy to do as he wished.[5]

The joys that are honoured today are the Annunciation, the Visitation of Our Lady to her cousin Elizabeth, the Birth of Our Lord, the Presentation in the Temple, and the Finding of the Child Jesus in the Temple.

Having established this interest in the joys of Our Lady, thoughts turned instinctively to the next subject of the rosary, for the realization that sorrow must accompany joy was borne constant testimony in their own harsh existence. They were deeply aware of the figure weeping at the foot of the Cross, and the example of holiness through suffering became in turn the subject of wrapt attention.

The title 'Our Lady of Pity' was in frequent use in England, meaning Our Lady of Suffering. Many churches had statues portraying Mary grieving over the body of her Son as He was taken from the Cross, and these were known as *Pietàs*.

In the thirteenth century, St Edmund wrote: 'You ought also to meditate on the most sweet Virgin Mary, with what anguish she was filled when she stood at the right hand side of her most sweet Son.'[6]

Suffering was no stranger in their lives, and her example brought a vision and inspiration mingled with consolation so deep as to be almost beyond human understanding. The sorrows were referred to as the 'Dolors of Our Lady', and on

Good Friday and Holy Saturday plays were enacted in many villages, with vivid portrayals of such subjects as Mary Magdalen's mourning and lamenting to St Joseph, and the scene at the sepulchre.

The great writers of the Church wrote at length on such subjects as Simeon's prophecy, and various forms of prayer concentrating on this aspect of the life of the Blessed Virgin are to be found in a small prayer book entitled 'Of the Compassion of Our Lady' which instructs the laity in a form of devotion that was easier to learn and recite than the full office. It consisted of a short lesson on the events in the passion and death of Our Lord, each one preceded by five Paternosters and five Aves. Each reading, together with the prayers, was to be said at different hours of the day, thus enabling the laity to pray the 'hours' as was the custom of the time, in the great religious houses.

The advantage of praying these particular mysteries in the form of the 'hours' lay in the sense of timing each subject with the actual hour of its happening in the day of Our Lord's passion, and they were written in verse and therefore easy to remember, finishing with the verse: 'Compline is the end of the day; and at the end of our life we have most need of Our Lady's help.'

The Sorrowful Mysteries of the rosary today differ slightly and are the agony of Christ in the Garden of Gethsemane, the Scourging at the Pillar, the Crowning with Thorns, the Carrying of the Cross, and the Death on the Cross.

Having dwelt on the passion of their Saviour, their thoughts then turned to contemplate the promise it held, and the happiness that awaited those whose lives had been lived in faith, hope and charity. They anticipated the return to the Garden of Paradise, and the presence of God, led there by their most gracious advocate, Mary the new Eve, free from all earthly suffering and reunited with their friends and all the saints whose protection they willingly acknowledged. All this was spelt out by the accounts in the New Testament of what came to be known as the five glorious mysteries of the rosary – the Resurrection and Ascension of Our Lord, the Descent of the Holy Spirit, the Assumption of the Blessed Virgin, and the Coronation in Heaven.

Through the influence of the many pilgrimages undertaken during the Middle Ages it was natural that movement and above all rhythm should become an important element of the rosary.

Much of the liturgy of the Church was intended to be sung, and the ave-psalm-psalter, as it became known, was no exception. Indeed, the word 'psalter' literally means a musical instrument of ten strings. Sometimes chanted within the lofty transepts of abbeys, on other occasions the psalter was sung in the open air by pilgrims on their way to one of the multitude of shrines dedicated to their most gracious Advocate. The universal popularity of pilgrimages in the Middle Ages had a profound influence on the element of rhythm and movement in the prayer of the rosary, and from the beginning Christians have acknowledged that there is a spiritual advantage in reciting the prayer in procession.

In those days, pilgrimages were a way of life, and the constant travelling to and fro across Europe to all the shrines of Christendom was never ceasing. The pilgrim was treated with great respect and honour, so much so that on one occasion during the wars against France in the fourteenth century an Englishman was taken prisoner in Cahors but released immediately when he managed to convince them that he was on his way to the shrine of Our Lady of Rocamadour.

The shrine of Our Lady of Walsingham was one of the most popular of the great centres of pilgrimage in the Middle Ages, and according to the historian Harrod, 'almost from the foundation of the priory to the dissolution there was one unceasing movement of pilgrims to and from Walsingham'.

Some of the shrines dedicated to Mary are of great antiquity, such as the chapel at Glastonbury which was reputedly founded when St Joseph of Arimathea came to England in AD 63, and legend has it that the wattles for the first chapel of Our Lady were made from his staff which took root when he thrust it into the ground. William of Malmesbury lists the many kings and others who sought to be buried there to await judgements under the protection of Our Lady. At the shrine of Our Lady of Storrington in Sussex, blessed by Pope Leo XIII, the Blessed Virgin was venerated as Our Lady of England, the only place using that title.

There were numerous shrines of less fame whose origins are often obscured by legend. There is frequently some difficulty in discovering precisely why a certain place was chosen, but it was usually in thanksgiving for blessings received or because a miracle was reported to have occurred in a certain place.

The people of the Middle Ages lived in an age that was not sceptical and they fully expected these things to happen, for most of these stories were prompted by a deep religious fervour that gave great gaiety of heart on the one hand, and on the other a profound sense of humility.

For the most part we have to rely on the chroniclers who usually saved their ink for the famous. In 1240 King Henry III sent an oak from the forest of Windsor to provide wood for the roof of the Chapel of Our Lady of Caversham, where the Benedictines had built a bridge across the Thames from the Abbey at Reading. This place of pilgrimage became very popular, and from the letters of Henry VIII we learn of an 'offering by the King at Our Lady of Caversham 18s. 4d' in September 1517 and another offering was made in 1520. In another volume of these letters Sir Robert Wingfield, writing to Wolsey in 1532, recounts 'this morning the King rode forth right early to hunt and the Queen is ridden to Our Lady of Caversham.' It was to be the last pilgrimage of Catherine of Aragon as recognized Queen of England.

In Wales the shrine of Our Lady of Pen-Rhys was much revered, particularly for its association with the rosary. Founded in 1179 it was built in rolling hills 1,000 feet above the Rhondda Valley, surrounded by the blue mountains. Llwellyn ap Hywell, a Welsh poet of the fifteenth century wrote 'a goodly place it is, with its summit and wooden slope, and the Virgin sanctuary beside the high forest. There is enthroned her image; there is pardeon to be gained in the five joys of Mary.' It was demolished by Cromwell in 1538.

A glimpse of the every-day working of these shrines is revealed by the list of bequests made by pilgrims and bene-factors. Of the many gifts laid at the foot of the altar, perhaps the most perplexing is the number of girdles. But further search reveals that it was the custom for a woman expecting a child to wear a belt inscribed with the Magnificat in hon-our of Our Lady and in the hope of a safe delivery.

One of the many examples of this is provided by Constance Bigod, who left her girdle worked with silver and gilt to Our Lady of Doncaster in 1449. In 1382 the Earl of Suffolk left a silver statuette of a fully armed man on a horse, perhaps to remind Our Lady that he was off to fight the French. Both instances demonstrate a marvellously practical approach and show how intimately this trust in Mary was woven into their lives.

At Doncaster the Carmelite friars founded their house in 1350 with the help of John of Gaunt, and through the years many pilgrims wound their way across the deep and treach-erous river to this shrine. Henry VII visited Our Lady of Doncaster on his way north after his coronation, as did his daughter Margaret on her progress to Scotland to marry James IV, and so the royal peregrinations continued.

The shrine of Our Lady of Doncaster was the subject of

widespread attention again in 1536 at the time of the Reformation. It was here that Robert Aske assembled some 30,000 followers under the banner of Christ, to meet the army sent by King Henry VIII. His followers were old soldiers, farmers and boys, all of whom had been brought up and educated by the monks, following the tradition of generations before them.

The monasteries were a familiar part of their lives, the places where their ancestors were buried, and the monks were their trusted and wise friends. The destruction of all that was familiar to them was incomprehensible and they felt justified in their protest. The King's anger erupted and many ended their lives on the gallows. But they were not forgotten, and today the statue of Our Lady of Doncaster is in the Lady Chapel of the Church of St Peter and St Paul in that town.

Perhaps the most telling of all memories of this great centre of medieval pilgrimage, when other events have faded into history, is the simple bequest of one Alice West: 'To Our Lady of Doncaster; my best bedes.'

Many of the shrines were dismantled during the time of the Reformation, and the accounts make sorry reading, for the custom of processing and worshipping at these holy places had become part of the English way of life. There are countless stories of the attempts made to preserve the remains, and in one place there is a bleak description of a procession of pilgrims encircling the charred ruins of their shrine in the moonlight while reciting the rosary in the chill night air.

Even today the strange circles seen sometimes etched on hillsides, too old for memories to recall, may well be the remains of early shrines. As processions reached their destination, the pilgrims fell to their knees and encircled the shrine in penance, and this custom was repeated within the precincts of large abbeys and cathedrals, forming well-worn circles from years of kneeling prayer.

The circle is so much part of our lives that we take for granted the influence that it has on almost all that surrounds us. Children with unerring instinct seek to join hands and form a circle of dance, and some people think that 'ring a ring of roses' comes from 'ring a rosary' with the 'atishoo atishoo' symbolizing the Holy Spirit at the Annunciation and at Pentecost. In Germany they sing '*ringel, ringel, rosen krantz*', 'ring a ring a rosary'.

The rhythm of the prayer of the rosary is reduced nowadays to the steady movement of hands on beads and the repetition of prayer, but in the early centuries prayer was held to be a physical as well as a mental exercise. The early Syrian hermits repeatedly threw themselves to the ground during their prayer, and their swollen knees and torn hands were the subject of much comment and admiration.

The Irish monks of St Patrick prayed with their arms outstretched in the form of a cross, known as the '*crossfigil*', and the original recitation of Our Lady's Psalter entailed fifty Aves, each one accompanied by a genuflection. King, later Saint, Louis of France 'knelt down every day fifty times, and in the evening and each time he stood upright, and then knelt down anew, and each time he then knelt down he said very slowly an "Ave Maria".'[7]

Although no doubt the main reason for these movements was the desire to make a total offering of mind and body to God, there must have been an element of keeping the mind alert, as a sentry on duty marches back and forth to keep his wits about him.

In the Middle Ages there was a great sense of movement in prayer, in a joyous and practical sense, and this is shown vividly in a popular legend of the time known as 'Our Lady's Tumbler'.

The tale describes the search of a renowned acrobat for a life of holiness and prayer within the Abbey of Clairvaux, and of his increasing sense of failure at his inability to pray with the same air of peace and serenity as those around him. Finding himself alone in the abbey church one day, he abandoned himself to joyful acrobatics. Peering around a pillar, his astonished fellow monks saw Our Lady, surrounded by angels, descending from the altar to approach their new brother with great joy. To the end of his day, the story relates, Our Lady's Tumbler danced his prayer and was much loved by his fellow monks.

This sense of rhythm is a vital part of the rosary, for the repetition of prayer creates a melodic background to the last and most important element of the prayer.

✢

The ave-psalm remained the form and style of Our Lady's prayer until the early fourteenth century and usually, especially in England, the Aves were repeated in honour of the joys, and hence their frequent name the 'gaudyes'. Increasingly the number of one hundred and fifty was divided into three fifties.

The third element of the rosary was the one which took the longest to develop, and it was not until the fifteenth century that meditation, rather than prayer in honour of a subject, became an accepted part of the rosary. In the legend of 'How Our Levidi's Sauter was first founde' Our Lady instructed her client to recite the first fifty in the morning in honour of the Annunciation, the second at noon in honour of the Nativity, and the third in the evening in honour of her Assumption and Glory in Heaven. At this stage there was no direct suggestion of meditation, rather the offering in honour of some specific subject.

Gradually the prayer developed into one of meditation, for Mary was named 'Our Lady of Wisdom', and in the rosary the story of the life of Our Lord is arranged by His mother for us to dwell upon following the example she gave, for 'His Mother Mary kept all these words, pondering them in her heart'.[8]

The word 'contemplation' comes from the Persian word *templum*, which was used to describe enclosures within their gardens, areas set aside for peaceful reflection, enclosed by immense hedges to enhance the impression of other-worldness, and it is apt that Our Lady's prayer of the rosary, the rose garden, should be one of devout recollection.

The length of time spent in prayer and meditation by monks and nuns of the early Church would be almost impossible to exaggerate, for every waking hour was spent in contemplation and worship of God. For people of the twentieth century whose constant cry is 'there is no time' it is a sobering thought to realize that these people quite literally gave their lives to God, for they considered that as man is made in the image of God, it is natural and right that the souls should turn at all times to its Creator. Not in the morbid way of the nuns of Tarrent, for whom the Bishop of Salisbury had written the *Ancren Riwle*, who were so enclosed that even their windows had to be the smallest and most narrow, covered in black cloth, but in the joyful way of St Francis of Assisi and St Clare. To them the birds, flowers, trees and sunlight were not luxuries but the word of God, as they were two centuries later to Fra Angelico whose meditative prayer is there for all to see, glowing from the walls of his Dominican monastery of San Marco in Florence. Fra Angelico wished to inspire the Christian beholder with a longing for the Garden of Eden, and he portrayed many of the subjects of the mysteries of the rosary.

As we gaze into his vision of the events of the life of Christ painted in great simplicity and purity of colour on the walls of the cells of his fellow monks, it is not difficult to imagine the incredulity of his brothers in the monastery as he moved from cell to cell. In each he painted a fresco which should be seen as a visual prayer and perhaps that is why they appear to be timeless. In fact only as an afterthought does the onlooker realize how immediately Fra Angelico viewed his subject;

thus Mary is seated peacefully on a monk's stool beneath the graceful arches of the cloister of San Marco when the angel Gabriel visits her. Far from displaying any sign of the dramatic news the angel has for Our Lady, his expression is one of devotion and peace, and the only indication given of his importance is in the brilliant rainbow of his wings, and even they are blended into the leafy shadows.

In the same way he often includes a brother monk with the saints in the scenes he depicts, as for example in the dramatic picture of the Holy Sepulchre. We see Mary and the holy women gazing into the empty tomb in statuesque amazement, and there behind the angel a monk smiles with such affection that we can only smile with him. In this sense of immediacy there was no lack of imagination but an awareness of the timeless quality of the events in the life of Christ which enabled Fra Angelico to see them all around him, in the peaceful cloisters in the heart of Florence, with an intimacy of prayer that was so much part of his own life of meditation, reminiscent of the legend of Our Lady's Tumbler.

The problem is not therefore one of discovering the time when meditation began to be part of the life of prayer but rather one of deciding when outside events so invaded the peace of the monastery that something had to be done to ensure that no greater encroachment could be made.

Probably that time came when the monks began to take on their work of illumination and writing, and still more when they went out into the world to teach.

The laity also needed some guidelines to help them, for although the Angelus bell continued to ring in every village in England until the time of the Reformation, there must have been many distractions.

In the fourteenth century a Carthusian monk, known as Dominic of Prussia, composed fifty *clausulae* or phrases to be added to the Aves, each one introducing a meditation on the life of Our Lord, and they follow the pattern of the meditations we have to this day. For example, for the Annunciation, he wrote: 'Hail Mary, full of grace, blessed be the fruit of thy womb Jesus Christ, Whom at the angel's word thou didst conceive of the Holy Ghost Amen.'[9]

From this came the expression 'Reading the Rosary', and it prompted the printing of many books on this method of reciting the rosary, usually illustrated with pictures to encourage meditation.

In 1328 a Dominican of Soissons in Northern France composed three books, each of which contained fifty legends or gaudia in honour of the Blessed Virgin, with instructions to 'remember' events in Our Lord's life, and rather mysteriously he wrote in the margin the words ROS or ROSARI rather than mention his own name. Another Dominican, Romeus de Livia, was reported to have held in his hands a knotted string on which to count his Aves, while he thought 'upon Child Jesus and His mother Mary'.

From this time the popularity of the rosary spread throughout Europe, and different Orders claimed varying arrangements of the prayer for their own. For example, the rosary of Our Lady of Consolation belongs to the Augustinian Order, and consists of twelve Paternosters and twelve Aves in honour of the twelve Apostles.

The Franciscan crown, as it is known, consists of seven Paternosters and ten Aves in honour of seven joys, and in the sixteenth century the Corona of Our Lady (frequently confused with the garland or chaplet of the rosary, but in fact quite separate) consisted of sixty-three Aves and seven Paternosters, to correspond with the sixty-three years of Our Lady's life.

The Corona was made up of six decades, with the three extra beads making up the pendant attached to the circle of beads, and this is thought to be the reason for those extra beads which rosaries carry today. Others think that these three are to be prayed for faith, hope and charity, to enable the rosary to be offered more devoutly.

The rosary in general use today is the Dominican rosary, which is made up of one hundred and fifty Aves, fifteen Paternosters and fifteen Glorias divided into three fifties. The wishes of those early English Christians expressed so clearly in the legend of 'Our Levedi's Sauter' have been faithfully followed, and the Joyful Mysteries are followed by the Sorrowful, and then the Glorious Mysteries of the life of Christ.

The element of rhythm, so vital a part of the rosary, is followed in the sequence of different mysteries which fall on different days of the week, and as the days run into months, the months to years, so the continual cycle of prayer is maintained, as it was decreed by Pope Pius V in the sixteenth century, and remains to this day.

Since Easter Monday is the Feast of the Angels at the Holy Sepulchre, Monday is thought of as the day of the angels, and the Joyful Mysteries are recited on Monday and again on Thursday. Tuesday, the day of apostles, and Friday, the day of the Crucifixion, are the days of the Sorrowful Mysteries.

The Glorious Mysteries are said on three days, on Saturday, traditionally the day of Our Lady, Wednesday the day of the Holy Spirit and Sunday the holy day of the week. Many people recite the entire Psalter daily but these are the days that have traditionally been held appropriate to the different subjects.

The origin of many of these devotions is to be found in this country and there is no doubt of their popularity, but it cannot be claimed that they were only in circulation in England.

The monks and abbots who helped to compose them were constantly on the move between the different houses of their Orders throughout Europe, and many of them came from the great abbey of Cluny in France and the Benedictine network which spread throughout Europe.

St Anselm, Archbishop of Canterbury, came here from Normandy and there were great exponents of Marian devotion in France, notably St Bernard of Clairvaux who was one of the first to break away from Cluny to join the newly-founded Cistercian Order, and his writings in the twelfth century are amongst the most eloquent ever composed on the subject of Our Lady.

In putting forward this notion that the rosary may well have roots in England, there is ample proof that England was truly the dowry of Mary, and that the devotion of the people was noted by their continental neighbours. This view seems to be confirmed by a report on the state of England in 1496 made by a secretary of the Venetian Embassy:

'They all hear mass every day, and say many Paternosters (rosaries) in public, the women carrying long strings of beads in their hands and whoever is at all able to read carries with him the Office of Our Lady: and they recite it in Church with some companion in a low voice, verse by verse, after the manner of the religious'.[10]

He must have felt the sight unusual enough to describe in such detail, almost with a sense of awe.

Throughout the story of the rosary, the figures whose actions affected the subsequent developments of the prayer and whose names recur are those of different Dominican monks, and much of the Dominican link with the rosary is prompted by the awareness of the importance of inward calm and recollection in prayer held by St Dominic. The Dominicans are the especial custodians of the rosary and St Dominic is undoubtedly the central figure in the story of Our Lady's Psalter.

✢

Chapter Three

Dominic was his name, whose work and worth
I publish, as the husbandman whom Christ
called to His Garden to help till the earth.

The Divine Comedy, Paradise Canto 111, Dante

✠

Almost any Catholic will tell you with unwavering certainty that the rosary was originated by St Dominic, adding something vague about the south of France, but both statements are misleading. There is no evidence that St Dominic invented the rosary, in fact all the evidence shows that as a means of counting prayers, this little circlet of beads was in use long before St Dominic appeared on the scene, and yet generations of devotees have clung happily to this belief while those with a detective's taste for facts have given themselves headaches over the whole issue.

The airy reference to the south of France is confusing too, for in the late twelfth century when these events took place, the area in question was nominally an English province through the marriage of Henry II to Eleanor of Aquitaine, taking its name of Languedoc from the language of the Troubadours in which *oc* instead of *oui* meant yes.

Over the centuries, in an attempt to satisfy the sleuths, enthusiastic Dominicans have produced 'evidence' of either miracles or certainly extraordinary coincidences, as if to pull a rabbit out of a hat, evidence such as the avalanche of roses that is said to have cascaded down upon the participants of the battle of Murat during the Albigensian Crusade.

On one occasion a document was found and said to provide definitive evidence, but the eager soul who, with touching enthusiasm, overlooked the difference between the words 'Dominus' and 'Dominicus' and thus exasperated late historians, with the result that most people dismiss the whole story for dependence on such flimsy evidence.

St Dominic was born in Castile, a land long used to producing Christian heroes. In the eleventh and twelfth century it formed the frontier of Christian defence against the Moor, its hills topped with stern fortified castles and villages, the last outpost of Christian Spain. St Dominic was born in the midst of this countryside, of noble parents whose record of service to their King and faith was impressive. Yet this stern land was renowned also as the land of ballads, where the troubadours sang their plaintive songs and Dante wrote dream-like verses about the strange beauty of the birthplace of the saint.

The formidable traits of heroic courage and gentle compassion were reflected in St Dominic's character. He was said to have been a serious child who grew into a man of ruthless severity with himself, and yet inheriting from his mother Joanna a great love of the poor and for those in need. Through all these different traits there shone a character infused with a love of God that brought a joy that affected his entire life.

Fortunately we have many accounts of St Dominic's appearance and personality from those who shared his life and work, given at the process for his canonization which took place less then fifteen years after his death.

His contemporaries describe him as a 'strong athlete' of Spanish appearance, and strikingly handsome, with great dignity of carriage and yet the most humble of men, capable of great physical endurance, whose fine features revealed his strength of purpose. In contrast to this rather daunting picture, these same people tell us of his humour and love of music, for he sang with gusto as he hurried along the dusty roads of France and Spain. His personal austerity was awesome and throughout his life he would eat only bread and drink water. He always insisted on sleeping on rough boards, driving to despair those who longed to care for him.

From the pen of his most beloved companion and successor as head of the Order, Jordan of Saxony, comes the most complete account of St Dominic. The phrases are short and direct, vivid with the pleasure and inspiration felt by all who shared his company, reaching undiminished across the centuries. He was always happy on his own account, and only sad out of sympathy with the sufferings of others, 'none was ever more joyous than he and none a better companion' are the words of his first biographer.

In the year 1200 he was subprior of Osma, having been ordained five years earlier, and in spite of the seclusion of this life of prayer and learning, his charm and prodigious knowledge quickly brought him to the attention of his fellow students.

In 1203 he was chosen to accompany his Bishop as a special emissary of the Pope on a visit to the Marches, and on their return from this journey the two passed through Languedoc for the first time. While they rested overnight in Toulouse, Dominic fell into conversation with their innkeeper who had recently joined the Albigensians. The dispute raged all night until by morning the exhausted publican, overcome by the persuasions of the fiery young priest, repented and returned to the Church.

This was the unlikely beginning to St Dominic's life of preaching, and, combined with the earlier arrival on the scene of one of the greatest statesmen of medieval Europe, Pope Innocent III, marked the first steps toward the eventual defeat of the Albigensian heresy.

The heresy was in fact as old as the hills, and owed its new name to the village of Albi in Languedoc, where its followers gathered in strength in the middle of the twelfth century, and their professed faith was Manicheeism with a new face but an unchanged character.

The teaching of Manes was based on the belief that all matter is evil and that man is a combination of two opposing principles – a spiritual being created by God, thrust into a material body created by an evil being. The most serious implication of this teaching was the denial of the two natures of Christ, for they refused to accept His Humanity while acknowledging His Divinity, and this in turn led to total rejection of the New Testament and any part of the Old Testament that did not agree with their teaching.

All beauty that surrounds man was seen, not as a gift of an indulgent Creator, but as the demonstration of evil from which escape was the only hope. All human love, itself a mirror of God's love, was obscured and abhorred, for it demonstrated to the heretic, man's reluctance to banish human ties.

Marriage was forbidden since its purpose was the procreation of children, and therefore the further imprisonment of spirit in matter. The ultimate release from evil was the deliverance of the soul, and if undertaken in the form of suicide this was greatly admired.

Since this way of life was somewhat daunting, and in fact placed the future of the human race in some doubt, the Cathari invented a kind of two-tier system. The inner sanctum of the 'Perfects' led this rule to the letter, while it was recognized that for lesser mortals who might already be married and leading normal lives, more modest but no less single-minded demands were made. From our viewpoint eight centuries later, it seems curious that an evil of such harshness could have held attractions, and the sweep of its success across the region seems incomprehensible.

However, the monastic orders were past their zenith, and the glories of Cluny were fading. The age that had seen the concentration of all learning within the monasteries, the creation of the most priceless manuscripts and illuminations ever seen, was gone. The means of ensuring the primacy of the Church as the seat of all learning, had become unwittingly the means of accumulating great wealth. The single pursuit of spiritual perfection had become lost as the monastic orders went out into the world to care for their new possessions, and the monks became by definition more worldly. The care for their most precious responsibility, the souls of their flocks, became lax and ineffectual.

In a more spiritual age man understood, even in this confusion, the unsatisfactory nature of worldly goods, and in the brilliant life of the courts of Languedoc where great wealth and indulgence held sway, amidst the revelry there was the uneasy feeling that all was not well. The priests to whom these people turned, half wanting but at least expecting admonishment and the teaching of more lasting values, were themselves too involved in the very things from which others sought escape. The spiritual guidance and forgiveness of sin were not forthcoming and this state of affairs made a fertile seedbed for the rigours of the heresy.

The wealth of the Church seemed immense and it was not long before envious eyes were turned upon such an Aladdin's cave. The nobles eagerly listened to the fierce strictures of the Manichees fulminating against the property of the Church, and the wild promise of land seizure was an irresistible lure to which their followers happily responded.

Although we think of the twentieth century as the scientific age to end all ages, when it came to learning, the people of the Middle Ages exhibited a far more scientific turn of mind. The wheatgerm theories of doing your own thing, or setting out on a voyage of self-discovery would have been incomprehensible and extremely distasteful to them. Theories of a purely logical nature were far more to their liking, and the universities were places where few facts were taught but the students acquired the ability to learn from a basis of logic, grammar and rhetoric. In this sense alone, the deceptively precise nature of the heresy held a fascination.

Lastly, but certainly not least, there was the promise of the *Consolatum*, a ceremony which promised the release of the soul to eternal happiness. If timed correctly in the last moments of life, all was well and lives of the utmost chaos and indulgence could be enjoyed until then. Raymond, Count of Toulouse, was known to travel everywhere accompanied by a 'Perfect' in case death should take him by surprise.

At first, the Church was slow to react and did so only in response to repeated demands from the populace, who in many cases took matters into their own hands. The cult was seen as a threat to society as a whole, dividing families and villages in the same way that in our century various freak sects have inflicted immense sufferings on the families of their followers.

Initially, the hierarchy seemed content to issue excommunications while the secular authority enforced exile and on occasion the confiscation of property, but there were times when an exasperated people acted alone, out of impatience with clerical leniency, and those they considered to be heretics were burned by enraged mobs.

This was the situation that awaited St Dominic when he returned to Languedoc, and he soon became a familiar sight travelling the length and breadth of the area. Others came to join him, not as yet bound by the rules of an Order, but united in their will to bring the word of God to anyone who would listen.

Meanwhile, since 1198 the papal legates had trodden a continuous path from Rome to Toulouse, some becoming increasingly overwhelmed by their task to the point where they begged the Pope to be allowed to return to the seclusion of their monasteries.

Those who did venture forth to face taunting crowds were few, and the sight that greeted the onlooker was startling. Long processions of lurching carriages wound their way through the dusty heat bearing the monks, who gazed with melancholy eye on the indifferent villagers while they paused to address in stentorian tones anyone who would listen, before the whole sorry caravan moved on to the next village. The contrast between this spectacle and the sight of their new

Albigensian 'saviours', with their long faces of self-denial, spoke oceans and needless to say the monks met with little success. The Pope was driven to saying bitterly that they were 'watchdogs who have lost their bark' and 'hirelings who abandon their flock to the wolves'.

This was the sight that greeted St Dominic and his followers on their travels. The anguish they felt at the sight of men abandoning their vocations was almost greater than the pity they felt for the flock so casually abandoned, for in their sorry state the clergy were more demoralized than corrupt and their preaching, such as it was, had been reduced to hazy admonishment.

St Dominic was thirty-three years old when he reached Languedoc. The next seventeen years were spent in ceaseless endeavour, establishing his Order of Preachers who were to go to the universities and become the foremost teachers of the age. Eventually his Order would travel to the four corners of the world teaching the words of Christ, not with loud denunciations but with brilliantly reasoned interpretation of the truths of the faith in words for all to understand.

In 1206 all that lay in the future, as St Dominic prepared for his mission in Toulouse. He realized the need for clear teaching above all, and he and his followers quickly rejected the luxury of the monasteries. Their own self-inflicted austerity, travelling bare-footed and in abject poverty from village to village, earned the reluctant admiration of the inhabitants.

In 1208 Peter of Castelnau, the Pope's legate, was murdered as he crossed the Rhone near Arles one evening, and this signalled the beginning of a war whose aims became increasingly confused. At times it was far more territorial and political than religious, as various factions seized the opportunity to settle feudal disputes and to take vast areas of land they had long coveted.

The crusade, launched by Pope Innocent III, set out in 1208, led by Christian forces from all over Europe. Despite some successes, which included the miraculous deliverance and victory against overwhelming forces at the walls of Muret in 1213, there were horrifying deeds of violence and brutality on both sides. The Crusade finally exhausted itself in 1215 with the death of its leader, Simon de Montfort.

Throughout the Crusade, St Dominic witnessed the carnage with growing disquiet, and made efforts to separate himself from those involved, for the cruelty with which the Albigensians were struck down was difficult to reconcile with Christianity.

St Dominic always took the opportunity to enter any church he was passing, for the chance to speak with his Lord was irresistible to the saint. On one of these occasions, tradition has decreed that Our Lady appeared to him in the church of Notre Dame de la Dreche. To comfort him in his sadness, the Blessed Virgin gave St Dominic her especial prayer of the rosary, with the instruction that this prayer should be offered by the people as an antidote to heresy.

The validity of this scene has been subjected to the most vigorous scrutiny down the centuries, and although not formally acknowledged by the Church, many wise heads have happily accepted the apparition of Notre Dame de la Dreche as a most apt beginning for the prayer of the rosary. Certainly it was apt that this saint should be credited by many with the founding of the rosary, not perhaps for any dramatic deed on his part but because the study of the life of St Dominic is in itself the perfect study of the prayer of the rosary, and his example gives us some understanding of the prayer Our Lady, on behalf of her Son, demands from us.

Sometimes it is felt that Dominic must have been in need of gentle admonishment for the length of his sermons, but that is the reaction of ordinary mortals; his whole personality was infused with a deep contemplative spirituality that lesser beings could scarcely begin to conceive.

Of all people, he understood that truth needs no embellishment, that wisdom, like the light that illuminates the world, is to be gained in understanding and not in rhetoric, and that understanding is only given through the power of prayer and meditation in the true silence of the soul. The foundation of that knowledge had been laid during his nine years in the peace of Osma in Spain, long before he reached Languedoc.

His prayer consisted of long periods of contemplation interrupted only by moments of speech, almost as if he were involved in deep conversation with his Lord. Sometimes his monks would see him thus in rapt attention, on occasion with his head to one side as if listening intently to someone who was addressing words of profound importance to him.

His love of prayer, usually sung, was infectious and he would exhort his friars to greater efforts with the words *Fortiter fratres!* as he paced along their choir stalls. Above all, the reciting of the Office afforded time for the prolonged contemplation of the mysteries and words of God. Anything that brought Christ more vividly to his mind was eagerly grasped and dwelt upon, such as the Sacraments or the beads of a rosary.

In his *Life of St Dominic* Father Bede Jarrett says,

'It was for this reason that the devotion of the rosary found in him its keenest apostle. His own way of prayer, consisting as we have seen of vocal expressions of love and adoration, was intermingled with silences; it passed from speech to contemplation as it fixed itself on to the character of Our Lord. All these elements were united in the rosary. It was contemplative and vocal.'[1]

The clearest illustration we have of this unearthly knowledge and familiarity with the life of the Saviour is portrayed by Fra Angelico, whose paintings seem like small windows to heaven.

Sceptics have often pointed out that if St Dominic was indeed handed the rosary by the Blessed Virgin, surely of all subjects to record, Fra Angelico would have found this one irresistible, and yet not once did he appear to find time to do so. The omission leads one to seek the true source of the Dominican link with the rosary if we are to be denied such neat proof. For St Dominic's influence on the development of the rosary was profound, and through his teaching this form of prayer its true worth and efficacy were realized for the first time, and it is for this reason that successive Popes have firmly placed the duty of the propagation of the rosary on Dominican shoulders.

The Dominicans became, above all, the preachers of the Church. Following the example of St Dominic, great knowledge, a dry and dusty commodity on its own, was to be distilled and brought to fruition by the power of prayer. St Dominic enveloped his monks in an austere spirituality with strict rules of chastity, obedience and poverty, not to draw acclaim from others in the manner of the Albigensians but to inspire them with the love of God. Their rhetoric, as they travelled around the universities of Europe was undoubtedly intellectual, but it was above all wisdom directed by prayer.

The events in the life of Christ and the example set by the life of the Holy Family as described in the New Testament, were the complete denial of the tenets of the Albigensian heretics, whose diatribes of hatred were in sharp contrast to the words of the Dominicans which were deepened by a true spirituality. Thus the Dominican insistence on meditation together with gentle repetitive words of adoration was given to the world as the example for the Christian to follow. We have come to know that prayer as the rosary.

The life of austerity and prayer became the inspiration to action, and St Dominic insisted on the most rigorous study from his followers. His love of learning and logic were legendary and books were the only luxury in the otherwise awesome simplicity followed by his friars. These things were to be treasured, not in themselves but as the essential weapons of a life devoted to preaching. One chronicler of the time noted that as the saint travelled to and fro across the wartorn plains of Languedoc, he was seen always with staff and book in hand.

When studying as a young man at Valencia, a great drought brought hardship and starvation to the farming people of the area, and Dominic, overwhelmed with compassion, sold all his books to help them. He seems to have made a habit of impulsively shedding all his books, with the result that he developed the ability to store wisdom within himself, thereby meditating on the matter of his reading and storing within a contemplative mind great tomes of knowledge. He made no secret of his wish to attract the most brilliant minds of the time to his Order, for in an age that was alive with speculation, he realized the need for lucid and exhaustive study.

However, his prodigious intellect had its drawbacks, for he never found need to commit any of his sermons to paper, and we have to rely on the accounts of those who heard him at the time, as he preached in the sunbaked fields or village squares of Languedoc. Those who witnessed these scenes were profoundly affected by the gentle insistence of that clear Castilian voice, and 'people were glad to hear him' is the simple verdict of one who was there.

In the course of his teaching St Dominic preached the form of prayer we recognize as the rosary. The division into fifteen different subjects on which to dwell, each one a different event in the life of Our Lord and the Blessed Virgin, combined with a suitable devotion, enabled him to instruct those who gathered to hear him. Though the prayer was never specifically named by St Dominic or those immediately around him, we have the evidence of one friar who joined the Order during the lifetime of the saint, and on whose prayer he undoubtedly modelled his own. Mention has already been made of Romeus de Livia, who was in the custom of meditating on the Blessed Virgin and the Child Jesus whilst reciting his Aves, counted with the aid of a knotted cord.

As the year 1215 progressed, the purpose of the Crusade gradually became buried in conflict, for the lenient terms of agreement set by the Pope served only to encourage the Albigensians to interpret such reason as a sign of weakness, and lack of confidence in the leadership of Simon de Montfort. St Dominic, alarmed at the menace to his new Order, returned to Prouille with his sixteen followers. After receiving their professions and blessing them, he explained his intention of dispersing his flock, 'hoarded, the grain rots; cast it to the winds, it brings forth fruit'.

Women too played an important part in St Dominic's work. Their adherence to his teaching became one of the great achievements of his ministry, and in fact his first religious house was founded for women.

One summer's evening in 1206, while the saint sat reading outside the gates of Fanjeaux, he looked across the valley in the fading evening light towards the line of black mountains in the distance. There he saw descending from heaven a globe of flame which hovered over the church of Prouille, and here he founded his first convent for women converted from amongst the 'perfects' of the heresy, and for many years the hill was known as the 'signadou', the sign from God. They were devoted to him, and Sister Cecilia, for one gives a glowing account of the saint in these words, 'he was always radiant and joyous except when moved to compassion by some misfortune or other of his neighbours'. There is a description of his return on foot from Rome, when on one occasion he brought back for each of his beloved sisters a small wooden spoon.

A rare glimpse of his humour is shown in a remark that he made to his biographer, Jordan of Saxony, in whom he confided his preference for speaking with young rather than old women, a passage that was deleted by the general Chapter of 1242.

It is sad that today St Dominic is so often identified with the Inquisition and little else. The first Inquisition was a secular affair and was set up several years before his time, for heresy was considered to be a crime against society. As time went on, the legal wrangles became increasingly acrimonious and for some the Inquisition became the means of removing political and personal enemies. Eventually, the Church stepped in to remove the trial of heretics to the ecclesiastical courts, but this was not until ten years after the death of St Dominic.

When the Dominicans were directed by the Pope to undertake this final act, they were extremely reluctant to do so and the Pope eventually commanded their obedience. Dominic's own life bore testimony to his dislike of force as a means of saving souls, and this was emphasized by his disenchantment with the Crusade. For the weapons of his personal war were spiritual and intellectual. On only one occasion was he known to have been present at the burning of heretics, and then according to Theodoric of Alpodia he rescued one of the victims from the flames. At the same time he displayed a strength of purpose that never faltered and his love of God and the Christian faith engulfed his entire life.

The years between 1215 and 1221 saw the saint continually on the move, organizing his various provinces, teaching without cease and praying at all times, especially when at last alone at the end of the day, when others had fallen asleep.

Eventually, in a state of exhaustion, he was overcome by fever when visiting Bologna in 1221. In an attempt to find relief for their saint from the heat of the city, his friars carried him up to the church of St Mary of the Hills. There he lay for several days in the cool beneath the terraces of vines, reflecting on his life and instructing his grieving brethren on the labours that lay ahead of them.

Finally realizing that death was near, he asked that he be taken back to Bologna, for he wished to be in the midst of his brotherhood, and there as they prayed together, he died on Friday, 6 August 1221.

The process for his canonization started only fifteen years after his death. During the time of his successor, Jordan of Saxony, the work of preaching found one of its greatest teachers, Albert of Cologne. His student, St Thomas Aquinas, completed the work started by St Dominic a century earlier, with a great shout of 'that will settle the Manichees' before the entire court of the King of France.

St Dominic's name is indelibly linked with the rosary and in a spiritual sense he was indeed the true founder of this prayer. Through the power of this small circlet of beads more was wrought than ever the sword could achieve, and that simple message of few words but profound meaning remains true to this day.

CHAPTER FOUR

'All night she sat in bidding of her bedes
And all day in doing good and Godly deeds.'

Spencer's *Faerie Queen*

The Dominican order spread rapidly. In 1221, the year of his death, St Dominic sent twelve friars to England, where they were greeted in Canterbury by Stephen Langton, then Archbishop. From there they travelled on foot to Oxford, arriving on the Feast of the Assumption to establish themselves east of St Aldate, where they built a chapel to Our Lady.

Almost immediately the work of preaching was started, and throughout the surrounding countryside the Dominicans became a familiar sight as they travelled from village to village gathering small crowds around them as people laid down their work to listen. Undoubtedly they preached the prayer of the rosary, if not by that name yet, at least in the form to which St Dominic attached so much importance, namely the contemplation of the events of the New Testament combined with the recitation of prayer. There is little doubt that this form of prayer was already familiar in the monasteries and probably to the communities in their immediate neighbourhood, and the 'black friars' went out into the fields and byways preaching the right of everyone, not merely those of the religious life, to this 'Little Office'. Their labours met with great success for by the end of the thirteenth century prayer beads had arrived, and they aroused such enthusiasm that even the monks were taken by surprise and eventually found cause to frown.

During the next century the growing popularity of the beads was not merely one of religious associations, and jewellers enjoyed a heyday as they explored endless possibilities for the use of precious stones and metals. Some of the descriptions of rosaries of the period read like tales from Aladdin's cave, and the makers of beads seemed happy to go to any lengths to satisfy the whims and fancies of the day. In the event they unwittingly added fuel to the flames of Lutheran disapproval and the hurricane of reform that ensued.

The next two centuries in England are interesting because it was during this time that rosaries became familiar objects, and this familiarity ran riot as nearly everyone sought not only to possess a rosary but in many cases to have a bigger and better one than his neighbour, until the Reformation put a stop to any such gaiety. By that time the prayer of the rosary and prayer beads were such an integral part of the life of a Catholic that their suppression was most acutely felt, and men were to die stubbornly refusing to submit to that suppression.

These were the years of the development of the rosary, a time that saw its tentative arrival followed by a period of acceptance, and an awareness of great spiritual value that threatened eventually to be eclipsed by luxury, and the events affecting that process are worthy of attention.

The word 'bead' comes from the Saxon verb 'bidden', to invite or pray, so that originally to 'bid the beads' meant simply to say one's prayers, for the word 'bede' meant prayer. Gradually the word bede, beade or bead came to refer to the small circle of wood or whatever material it was, for it represented a prayer and so that word was quite appropriate. Not until the end of the sixteenth century was all religious association removed, and the round sphere through which a chain was threaded to form a necklace retained the earlier name.

The use of beads as a mnemonic device was by no means the exclusive right of the Christian. The Crusaders had already discovered Muslims using exotic counting beads, and some writers seem to find a definite link between the appearance of prayer beads in Europe in the twelfth and thirteenth centuries and the Crusades to the Holy Land. In 1272 a monumental slab was carved to decorate the tomb of one crusader, Frère Gerars of the Knights Templar in Liege, and he is portrayed with beads in hand.

At the same time, Marco Polo was encountering the King of Malibu on his travels and discovering that the King

'. . . wears also, hanging in front of his chest, from the neck downwards, a fine silk thread strung with 104 large pearls and rubies of great price. A reason why he wears this cord with 104 great pearls and rubies is (according to what they tell) that every day, morning and evening, he has to say 104 prayers to his idols such is their religion and their custom.'[1]

Some three centuries later, St Francis Xavier was surprised to find that rosaries were familiar to the Buddhists of Japan. For the Christian the search to find a means of keeping tally with his prayers had begun centuries earlier when the first monk hermit, St Paul, left his home in Egypt and fled from the confusion of the world. There in the desert he found shelter in a cave used previously by the money-makers of Cleopatra's time, and near his new home there flowed a spring beneath a palm tree, thus, as the story of his life neatly comments, he was provided with drink and clothing. While time and custom carry him light years from today, his longing to find some means of counting his prayers and thereby gaining a sense of achievement are familiar enough, and each day he gathered three hundred pebbles which he passed through his fingers as he prayed.

His first life story was written by another hermit of the desert, St Jerome, of whom there is a portrait in the National Gallery. He is portrayed seated on a rock in the desert, praying and fingering a primitive circle of beads while a lion sleeps peacefully by his feet.

In their solitude, time can have had little reality or importance. These simple means of counting provided anchors of stability in a life that threatened to dissolve in a haze of light and sanctity, and evidence has been found that these devices were carried to the grave.

Such were the means of keeping a tally of prayers until eleventh century Europe awoke from a century of Viking invasion to the time of greatest glory in the history of the monasteries, and the focus of this achievement was the great monastery of Cluny in France. In the words of one of the first monks, 'it was a valley shut off from all contact, which breathed such a perfume of aloofness, repose and peace, that it seemed like a heavenly solitude'. In the midst of this heavenly solitude the abbey of Cluny was built, and within its pale walls the community lived in strict observance of the Rule laid down by St Benedict four centuries earlier.

The community that gathered in this renowned centre of Western monasticism was made up of monks and lay brethren known as the *conversii*. The monks remained for the most part within the abbey, leading a life devoted to the liturgy and the constant search for sanctity prescribed by the Rule, while the *conversii* undertook the practical and domestic duties of the monastery. However, all attended the daily recital of the office laid down by St Benedict and this included the recital of the 150 Psalms.

The lay brethren or *conversii* were usually illiterate, and to memorize the entire Psalter was beyond them. To enable them to take part in the prayer of the community they were allowed to recite the appropriate number of Paternosters with the help of a knotted string. People from the neighbouring villages, summoned by the great Monastery bell, followed the example of the *conversii*, and thus was launched with practical simplicity the tradition of reciting 150 prayers with the aid of a string of beads, or in this case, knots.

Because prayers were originally counted in this way, prayer

beads were often referred to as a 'pair of Paternosters' or simply 'Paternosters' and the people who recited them were referred to as 'Paternosterers'. The gentle sound of their repetitive prayer has often been cited as the source of our expression 'pitter-patter'.

The peace and holiness of Cluny became the inspiration for great learning, and the monks restored much of the knowledge damaged or abandoned during the dark centuries leading up to their own. Their exquisite illuminations awakened a longing for and a recognition of beauty and their influence was widespread.

In 1041, soon after the founding of Cluny, we read from the writings of William of Malmesbury in England that Lady Godiva was bequeathing a 'circle of threaded jewels upon which she was wont to number her prayers to be hung about the neck of the Blessed Virgin's image in the church at Coventry'. This was long before St Dominic could have 'invented' the rosary, and so it is safe to assume the Lady Godiva only used her jewelled beads to count her prayers, and yet the instruction that her beads be bequeathed to the statue of Mary implies a devotion and gratitude for favours received. As this coincided with a spread of devotion to Our Lady in Europe, it therefore seems likely that the prayers she counted were Ave Marias, and not the Paternoster as was the custom.

One of the effects of the Cluniac influence was that from the twelfth century until the end of the fifteenth, art was looked upon as one of several forms of worship and as a visual addition to man's understanding of the scriptures. Most of the illuminations and masterpieces created before the Renaissance are the work of anonymous monks who looked beyond this world for their reward. Their sense of proportion and humility dictated that time spent in such labour was immaterial, and hour after hour, year in year out, the laborious and exquisite work progressed as a continual prayer. With great love and painstaking attention, glowing borders of jewel-like flowers and birds were painted on parchment to surround the faces of the saints; art for art's sake in the complete sense of the word. When old age and infirmity eventually slowed the hand at work, the aged monk handed his pens and brushes to a younger man who took up the task. Such things as deadlines or the vagaries of a fickle patron were totally unknown to him.

The effect on the laity was obvious, and it is hard for us in the twentieth century to understand the volume of output in works of art which were created for the glory of God. All the artistic energy which is today poured into creating songs or films, in the days of Cluniac influence was directed solely towards the embellishment of the liturgy, the illumination of priceless manuscripts or the architecture of great abbeys; rosaries were not left out of this new awareness and they became increasingly beautiful.

Seen in this light, the jewelled beads of the time fit quite naturally into an overall picture of the exuberant worship of God, for all this activity came before the pall of Puritan austerity had descended, when all that was grey and severe was considered fit for a God Who in return gave man a world of light and beauty.

Thus the rosary beads were added to the luggage of the Christian pilgrim, and they became the object of attention as if seen for the first time in the new light of discovery. Not only were beads of practical use, but as they assisted the quantity of prayer so the quality of this renewed fervour was reflected in more tangible form. Beads became not simply knots of twine, but jewels strung on exquisite threads of gold fit for a king's ransom.

In this respect Christian beads bore an uncanny resemblance to those beads of other cultures and religions, but for all that they were different. The reason lay not so much in their ornate quality as in the manner in which they differed from other prayer beads which had been in use before them – the great beads of the King of Malibu or the strange and exotic beads seen by the Crusaders to the lands of Saladin in the East – and that essential difference lay in matters spiritual. For the beads of a Catholic are blessed by a priest and as such they become an instrument of grace in direct relationship to the person for whom they are blessed. There is a prayer from the Old Sarum rite which was used in Saxon England for the blessing of beads which includes the words:

'Whoever endeavours by means of these (beads) to honour by holy service the most Blessed Mary, Mother of God, may her Son our Lord Jesus Christ return him great things for small; may He accept his devotion, forgive him his sins, fill him with faith, indulgently succour him, mercifully protect him, destroy whatever is adverse to him, and grant him what is prosperous.'

The importance of the individual in relation to the beads that are blessed is underlined by an incident that occurred at Lourdes during the apparitions of Our Lady to St Bernadette in 1860. There was in St Bernadette's class a girl who wished her rosary to be blessed by 'the Lady' and she entreated Bernadette to exchange her beads when next she visited the grotto. With misgivings Bernadette did so. When Our Lady appeared she hesitated and her lips moved, 'That is not your rosary', she murmured. Bernadette explained and the vision receded, saying 'Where is your own?' Bernadette hastily turned and grasped her own beads from the hands of her friend.

There could be no clearer instruction from a more august source of the importance attached to the beads themselves. No other article has been singled out for such attention, and it is an indication of the power for acquiring grace and spiritual happiness which is encompassed by this ring of beads, and the great joy to Mary when this prayer is recited in her honour.

This sense of reverence is underlined by the custom in many countries of people being buried with their beads resting in their hands. In the days when great monuments were carved on the tombs of the deceased it was quite usual that the adornment of the figure should include a rosary.

In the *Monumenta Vestuta* is a plate showing an effigy of Richard Patten carrying at his waist a purse, a dagger and a rosary, being thus ready for anything.[2] One of the oldest examples of this custom is to be seen in Paris on the tombstone of the Dauphin Humbertus, who became a Dominican and died in 1354, in which two of the Dominicans included in the carving carry rosaries.

The fourteenth century has been called the calamitous century, and in all the turbulence chroniclers seem to have found little time for gentle ruminations on prayer beads, but events were taking place that were to have far-reaching effects on the years to come. The Hundred Years War between England and France brought, as a side effect, a sense of nationalism dividing the old European unity which meant so much to Catholicism. The Black Death swept through Europe wreaking devastation on the population, and in Montpelier alone, of St Dominic's 140 monks only seven survived, and such was the feeling of despair that one Irish monk wrote: 'I leave parchment for continuing the work if any of the race of Adam survive this pestilence.'

The great chronicler Froissart appears as immune to human suffering as any journalist, for he remarked briefly that 'a third of the world died'. In Paris it was noted that swearing and gambling had diminished to such an extent that those engaged in the making of dice were turning their products into beads for 'telling Paternosters'. Whether to increase their profits or to benefit their souls it is hard to say.

In England the effects of the plague were equally devastating, and the effect on the monastic orders was dramatic, greatly reducing their numbers while the monasteries retained the wealth their scholarship and stewardship had unwittingly gathered. All these seemingly unrelated events were profoundly to affect the years that lay ahead, but the immediate future seemed to bring a temporary calm and a respite in the remorseless train of events, and with it an air of near frivolity.

Wooden beads were once more forgotten while the popularity of ornate rosaries seemed to know no bounds. To cater for the flourishing new industry, the bead-makers installed themselves in London in the shadow of St Paul's Cathedral, and the streets became known as Pater Noster Row and Ave Maria Lane. A London jeweller of the time, one Adam Ledyard, had in his stock Paternoster beads of white and yellow amber, coral, jet and silver, and Ave beads of jet and blue glass as well as cheaper sets of maple and white bone for children. Meanwhile in Paris business was equally brisk for there were three guilds of bead-makers, each specializing in different materials. It is interesting to note that all the amber which was so popular was supplied solely by the Knights Templar from their vast estates in East Prussia.

Much criticism has been heaped on the immense fortunes spent on ecclesiastical adornment in the Middle Ages, and the whole question of opulence versus simplicity is a vexed one. In a sense, each age produces different reactions which vary according to the prevailing sense of values. In the Middle Ages, people clearly understood that prayer was more powerful than money, and material comfort was scarcely considered for it was little enjoyed even by the wealthy. Man appears to have paid far more attention to his soul than his body and evidently found it entirely satisfying to do so, for it remained the norm until the Reformation. They took to heart the words of the Gospel, that 'where your heart is, there also will be your treasure'. Since their interest lay in God and His Church, it seemed appropriate that their efforts should be concentrated in that direction.

The view was held that the spiritual welfare of a man was his first consideration, and a trouble-free life was the gift of a benevolent God. This emphasis on the importance of the spiritual life is borne out in wills of the time, when much time and thought is given to spiritual matters, and practical considerations of property are treated as afterthoughts with great expedience.

The will of Sir Thomas Wyndham in 1521 is a typical example. After at great length exhorting those who remained to pray for his soul he makes elaborate and lengthy arrangements for a thousand masses to be said at different times, and in different chapels. Only after all spiritual matters have been considered, does he turn briefly to the distribution of his property. Sometimes the wills show a commendable ingenuity in mixing the practical and sacred in one instruction. When the Alderman of York died in 1506 he granted his house to his wife as long as she remained unmarried, and held each year at Candlemass a dinner for thirteen men and one woman 'in honour of Christ and His twelve apostells and ye woman in ye worshippe of oure Ladye and to kepe our Lady Masse wekely on ye Saturday.'[3]

It becomes obvious that prayer, and often prayer in the form of the rosary, is one of the great concerns of a man's life, and therefore beads ranked high in the list of beloved possessions to be handed down, often being treated as heirlooms by the recipient.

The families of Yorkshire are happily well documented and the examples are too numerous to list. One family in particular offers a glowing example, not only for the beauty of their wills but for the finely detailed portrait that emerges of a noble and Christian family of England of the time.

In 1401, Richard Scrope, Lord of Bolton, left his son a 'pair of paternosters of coral' and two years later his kinsman

Roger, Lord Scrope, left to his son and heir 'my pair of Paternosters of coral with a jewel of gold which belonged to my lord, my father; also a cross of gold which I usually carry about with me'.[4] In 1451 Lord John Scrope asks in his will that '24 poor men clothed in white gowns and hoods each of them having a new set of wooden beads' should pray on them at his funeral at Scrope's chapel within the Cathedral of York. He adds that these poor men may stand or sit at will. This request is not as strange as it might appear for it was quite common for people to pay others to bid their beads for them, particularly when they required all fifteen decades to be said daily, and these people were referred to as bedesmen. Sometimes they too were left money in gratitude for services rendered during the lifetime of the deceased.

In 1488 Agnes, daughter of Lord Scrope, was left by her mother-in-law 'a pare of bedes of golde', and in 1498 the will of Lady Anne Scrope sparkles with the jewels she carefully leaves to members of her family and household. One of her rosaries (she leaves three others of coral) is of sufficient value to merit breaking into decades, illustrating the sad fate that befell nearly all the priceless beads of the time: 'To the rood of North door (St Paul's in London) my heart with gold with diamond in the midst. To Our Lady of Walsingham 10 of my great beads of gold and tasselled with the same. To Our Lady of Peue (Westminster) 10 of the same beads. To St Edmund of Bury 10 of the same beads. To St Thomas of Canterbury, 10 of the same beads. To Thomas Fincham 10 Aves and 2 Paternosters of the same beads.'[5]

Other wills offer examples of the strange habit, in our eyes, of bequeathing clothing as well as beads to various shrines, but that is to misunderstand the purpose of such gifts, for many of the ornate vestments of the period were made from such bequests. Thus the will of Dame Catherine Hastings must have been greatly valued:

'To Our Lady of Doncaster my tawny chamlett gown. To Our Lady of Belcrosse my black chamlett. To Our Lady of Hymmymburgh a pece of cremell, and a lace of gold of Venyss sett wt perle. To my moder my best bedes. To my sister Margerette a pare of beides of whitt jasper. To my niece Agnes a pare of beides of coral.'[6]

Some wills are more obviously practical and to the point like that of Nicholas Aglionby of 1505: 'I bequeth to old John Chapman my carlill dagger and a pare of bedes of yalow box.'[7]

One of the remarkable facts to be gleaned from these wills is the apparent variety of stones used by jewellers of the time. Silver and silver gilt emerge as the most popular metals for the chain, and often the Paternoster bead or gaud as it was often called, as in the will of Dame Joan Chamberleyn who leaves 'a payr of coral baydes gaudiett wt silver' and Dame Agnes Clifton who leaves 'my sonne's daughter a pare of rown curi-all bedes gaudiett wt silver gilt.'

Gold was also popular, as in the rosary John of Gaunt leaves: 'A chain of gold of the old manner with the name of God in each part, which my most honoured lady and mother the Queen, whom God pardon, gave me, commanding me to preserve it, with her blessing; and I desire that he (his son Henry, later King Henry IV) will keep it, with the blessing of God and mine.'[8]

Charles the Bold was said to have inherited some thirty-five rosaries of coral, crystal, gold and endless other precious jewels and the makers appear to have been carried away on a tide of richesse.[9]

Although seen in the kindest light, on most occasions the intention was to make this instrument of prayer as beautiful in material terms as they wished the prayer to be spiritually, it is difficult not to feel on some occasions that they overdid things. The Princess Elector of Brandenburg had in her dowry a Paternoster of gold set with pearls, rubies, emeralds and diamonds, much to the envy of the English ladies of the court. Some were made of coral, which was said to bring good luck, and others were of an immense length. In 1488 the King of Scotland inherited from his father the 'grete bedis' of 122 beads and a tassel, all of gold.[10]

Add to this great size the growing habit of attaching all manner of brooches, rings and cameos, it is a wonder that they did not project themselves into the next life by falling over their rosaries.

Chaucer remarked on this new habit of attachments in his description of the Prioress:

She wore a trinket on her arm
A set of beads, the gaudes tricked in green
Whence hung a golden brooch of brightest sheen
On which there first was graven a crowned A
and lower: *Amor vincit omnia.*[11]

Some time later, Sir Thomas More was obviously amused by the new fashion for in his apologue of the wolf who went to confession to the hypocritical fox he says 'his confessor shook his great pair of beads upon him almost as big as bowls.'[12]

While all this exuberance held sway, the actual prayer of the rosary was in danger of sinking without trace, and counting the beads threatened to become a profitable pastime in financial rather than spiritual terms. Rosaries which had initially been an 'outward sign', had slipped into the culture of the time, with strange and diverse roles ranging from being an essential part of a wedding trousseau, to becoming a status symbol as a gift, and eventually being worn in every way possible, even as a necklace.

When all hope of a return to the real purpose of prayer beads appeared almost lost, there came on the scene a fiery Dominican from Brittany named Alanus de Rupe, who made it his main purpose in life to restore the prayer of the rosary.

Taking one glance at the situation and using what was to become typically picturesque language, he exhorted his fellow preachers to be like 'Noahs making an ark for their brethren' and 'Jacobs raising ladders to heaven', and in 1475 with another Dominican, Joseph Sprenger, he founded the Confraternity of the Rosary. So great an impact did this man make that while some regarded him as a hot-head and a trouble-maker and others as a saint, many people felt that he was the true founder of the rosary since it was he who made known the apparition of Our Lady to St Dominic so many years before.

There is little doubt that his preaching was persuasive, and the popularity of the Confraternity of the Rosary spread rapidly throughout Europe. Membership entailed no rigours other than the promise to recite the rosary each week, endorsing the promise by signing a book of enrolment, and it quickly sought and received papal approval.

The tragedy was that there were not more like him, for by the second half of the fifteenth century every Catholic who was alive to the situation was clamouring for reform. However, they were overtaken by events which even the most pessimistic of their number could not have foreseen.

In England the effects of the Reformation are well known, and with hindsight it is possible to fix precise dates, while in practice events unravelled gradually and the unexpected forced awareness.

An ironic example of this is provided by William More, Prior of Worcester. In 1530 Lady Sandys, a favourite of Henry VIII, sent William a 'peyer of grete amber bedes of 5 settes'. She proved a loyal friend for later she wrote to Cromwell on his behalf when More was under house arrest for treason. He was in trouble again some years later for his great extravagance.

But this charge of extravagance became an overworked scapegoat for what followed, and the overall image of a

Church weighed down by material wealth was used as reason enough for what amounted to legalized vandalism, and much of English heritage was destroyed in the effort.

Until his meeting with Anne Boleyn, Henry VIII was known for his great devotion and loyalty to Rome and the shrine of Our Lady of Walsingham in particular was visited several times by the King. In 1510 he went there on pilgrimage, walking the last stage of the journey bare-footed, and he presented the statue of Our Lady with a valuable necklace.

It is said that years later as he lay dying he was overheard praying to Our Lady of Walsingham. His rosary is of particular interest because of its intricate composition. Like many prayer beads carried by men, it consisted of one decade only, and the ten Aves and one Paternoster hung from his belt. Made in fine boxwood, the Paternoster bead opens to reveal an intricately carved scene from the Mass of St Gregory with the Virgin and Child enthroned in glory, the same bead being carved with the king's name and royal arms. Known as the Chatsworth rosary, it can be seen today in the home of the Duke of Devonshire.

While Henry laid waste the monasteries of England, his uncle by marriage, the Holy Roman Emperor, was battling with the reformers in the Netherlands. Charles V was a man of great holiness, and in complete contrast to the custom in England, he carried a simple rosary of wooden beads as a sign of his humility. The wars increased and overwhelmed him to such an extent that he eventually hurried away to a monastery to escape the complexities, which he offloaded onto his son, Philip II.

With the marriage of Philip to Mary Tudor, there was great hope in England for a return to the old faith but in the event this turned out to be shortlived.

As beads had of old been a sign of penance when worn by pilgrims, so now they became a different sort of sign; William Cecil, the architect of the Reformation under Henry VIII, is said to have averted the fury of Mary Tudor by parading his prayer beads before the Queen. Another account describes Mary Tudor riding through the city of London and 'After her threescore of gentlemen and ladies everyone havying a payre of bedes of black' and on another occasion she purchased a 'Payre of bedes of gold enamelled black and white'.[13] The bead-makers of Paternoster Lane breathed again. Alas, not for long, for the days when the monks frowned disapprovingly on the laity with their dazzling prayer beads were gone forever.

The reformers themselves unwittingly underlined the importance and sanctity of rosary beads for the mere possession was enough to forfeit a man's life. In the reign of Elizabeth I one Thomas Atkinson was convicted of being a priest on the sole evidence of beads found in his possession and he was taken to York and hanged, drawn and quartered. He was over seventy years of age at the time.

A new type of rosary was needed that took little space, freed from the rhythmic clicking of beads and immediate recognition.

The Knights of Malta wore a form of rosary ring on their sword belts, and it was this ring that found its way into use in England during the persecutions. The rosary ring is a small cogwheel with ten knobs for the Aves and a cross for the Paternoster and Gloria. It is easily worn on a finger and turned by the thumb and has been used over the years by Christians in wartime.

There is, however, one fine rosary left to us from those troubled times. When Mary Queen of Scots was led to her death in 1587 she carried in her hand her golden rosary, until her executioner stepped forward to claim his traditional right to the adornments of the condemned. Her servant Jane Kennedy protested, and on the Queen's plea, the rosary was saved. Jane Kennedy eventually gave it to the Queen's friend Anne Dacre, wife of Philip, Earl of Arundel, and the beads can be seen at Arundel Castle today. The second rosary, which Jane Kennedy was unable to rescue and which the Queen had worn, was eventually burnt.

Of the many stories told of Mary Queen of Scots one is particularly apt. It appears that when she sailed from France to Scotland as a young woman, she brought with her the first sycamore trees to reach these islands, for there is a legend that as the Holy Family fled into Egypt, they rested beyond the city of Hermopolis in a grove of sycamores, and these trees have held people's imagination ever since. Perhaps those devoted members of Mary Queen of Scot's household may have carved their prayer beads from these first sycamore trees.

Because of its association with the Holy Land, olive wood has always been considered suitable for rosaries, but beads can and have been made of anything from knots to rubies and there have been some strangely exotic materials used. St Theresa of Avila wore a rosary made from dried rose petals worked into the form of beads, and as she walked along the cloisters of her Carmelite convent she was followed by the sweet scent of roses and this connection is sometimes claimed as the source of the word rosary. Appropriately, the Dominicans have in their care surely the strangest of all, for in the monastery of St Sabina in Rome there is a rosary the beads of which are tiny dried and blackened oranges from a tree said to have been planted by St Dominic, for this monastery has been the headquarters of the Dominicans since 1222.

After the Restoration when Catholics were free once more to practise their faith, the rosary quietly took its place in the overall liturgy of the Church, the days of childish carefree exhibitionism gone for ever and a new maturity emerged in its stead. The days of the bead-makers of Paternoster Row and Ave Maria Lane are long gone, and the last bombing of Hitler's Luftwaffe in 1944 did extensive damage to the area, although the street names survive.

Today prayer beads are mainly made of wood or glass and

come from far and wide. There are only a few rosaries made in England. Most beads are made in Italy or in Ireland, and the Czech Republic is by far the biggest producer of beads in the world.

But the beads are only as important or valuable in the true sense as the prayer they count, for the rosary is there to lead men to think, to lift up their eyes to the hills, to Him 'Who dwells in the heavens', and if there were no beads we could still do worse than imitate Robert Winchelsey, Archbishop of Canterbury in the fifteenth century, who 'no sooner was he free from business than he used at once, wherever he might be, to begin counting the Angelic Salutation on his fingers.'[14]

✠

CHAPTER FIVE

And the Pope has cast his arms abroad for agony and
  loss,
And called the kings of Christendom for swords about
  the cross,
The cold queen of England is looking in the glass;
The shadow of the Valois is yawning at the Mass;
From evening isles fantastical rings faint the Spanish
  gun,
And the Lord upon the Golden Horn is laughing in
  the sun.

Lepanto, G. K. Chesterton

While the events of the Reformation continued their remorseless progress in northern Europe, events in the south took place that were to ensure that the name of Lepanto would always be associated with Our Lady's prayer.

It was at a time in history when Christian Europe stood in grave danger of being overrun and subjugated to the power if Islam, and the dark foreboding cloud whose shadow had increased over the centuries now seemed to threaten Christians to the point where their days seemed numbered.

In practical terms, Europe was in no state to withstand the concerted force that stood poised at its gate. That it did so was due in large measure to the power of the prayer of the rosary as the last knight of Europe came crusading across the seas with the fleets of Christian Europe in his wake. It was the last triumphant sea battle against Islam guided, suitably enough, by another Dominican saint, Pope Pius V.

Far from the plains of Languedoc, across the Adriatic Sea and beyond the Isthmus of Corinth lies the bay of Lepanto. It was here that the greatest sea battle in history was fought on 7 October, 1571. The events which led to this auspicious day had their beginnings far away on the plains of Arabia in the early part of the seventh century, when a young camel-driver emerged from the desert to be acclaimed as the Prophet of Allah. From that day forth Islam was on the move.

By the end of the Prophet's life, by persuasion or the sword, all Arabs had been compelled to accept Islam, wave upon wave of Mogul warriors sprung from the Arabian plains to strengthen the arm of Muhammad's successors, whose sword carried the fight throughout the eastern Mediterranean and into North Africa.

The full horror dawned painfully on the Christian world when in 638 Caliph Oman, Muhammad's conquering successor, rode into Jerusalem on a white camel and the holy lands were lost.

Spain succumbed to Islamic rule in 712 and the invading forces swiftly crossed the Pyrenees reaching as far north as Poitiers, and as Gibbon observed: 'a victorious line of march had been prolonged above a thousand miles of the rock of Gibraltar to the banks of the Loire; the repetition of an equal space would have carried the Saracens to the confines of Poland and the highlands of Scotland.' Only the great victory of Charles Martel in 732 arrested their progress.

Gradually the Christian world raised itself, as if from a trance. The Crusades were marshalled by Pope Urban to recapture the holy lands and were undertaken by Christians from all parts of Europe. Their success was limited but the progress of Islam was temporarily halted and invasion of the West averted.

After a brief respite, the Turkish Empire steadily increased in power and might until the sixteenth century. On land their armies were made up of fighting men, or janissaries as they were known, whose success in battle was renowned, for they placed no value whatsoever on their own lives, still less on others, and obeyed orders instantly. In the Mediterranean the power of the Turks in the Islamic world had forged a cohesive and dauntingly invincible enemy, uniting squabbling factions under one sovereign, Suleiman the Magnificent, of legendary and cynical cruelty.

There was just one minor irritation in an otherwise idyllic state of affairs for the Sultan. Since their expulsion from Rhodes by the Turks in 1565, the Knights of St John had made their home on the Island of Malta. From there they ventured forth as corsairs, constantly teasing and snapping at the tail of the huge dragon that was the Turkish fleet, as it plied to and fro on the direct route from its base in Constantinople to Tripoli in North Africa. Every relief ship sent by the Turks ran the risk of being intercepted and destroyed by the Knights, and this was not to be tolerated by the man who considered himself the undisputed Emperor of East and West.

Forewarned by their agents in Constantinople of increased activity in the dockyards and arsenals, the Knights were prepared in some measure when the huge fleet of the Infidel sailed into sight, the personal standard of Suleiman the Magnificent glinting in the Mediterranean sun, surmounting the largest and most beautiful ship that was ever seen on the Bosphorus. This was the flagship of Piali, Admiral of the Fleet under Mustapha Pasha, whose life-long ambition it was to expel the Knights of Malta from the Mediterranean once and for all.

Vastly outnumbered by the Turks, the Knights fought valiantly under their Grand Master, Jean de la Vallette, in a siege that has become a legend of heroism. When the humiliated Turkish fleet finally withdrew in September they left fewer than 600 Knights alive on the Island, while of 40,000 Turks, only 10,000 survived.

With hindsight it became clear that the Knights of Malta, who from their inception had pledged themselves to war against Islam, had by this victory taken the first step in the eventual defeat of their enemy. At the time, their triumph appeared heaven-sent in the eyes of those few battle-worn survivors, but to Christian Europe, which had watched with resigned pessimism at the outset and gradually with disbelief and elation, the outcome was nothing short of miraculous. To the Turk, it was a humiliating and unforgiveable blow to the pride of Islam, but by no means a mortal blow, and the arsenal of Constantinople was seething with activity as the work of rebuilding the fleet began with heightened urgency. For retribution at its most terrible was the certain outcome of the crushing wound inflicted by the Knights of Malta on the all-important prestige and pride of Suleiman the Magnificent.

The one man who saw quite clearly that an immense conflict of greater consequence than all that had gone before was imminent, and that something extraordinary was needed if Europe was to be saved, was deep in prayer in the shadows of his private chapel in the Vatican.

The man who assumed the task of stemming the Islamic tide on the one hand, and of strengthening the nerve of the quaking Christian princes on the other, was not a bellicose statesman of great political prowess, but a monk of humble origin upon whom the mantle of the papacy fell. He was a Dominican thoroughly schooled in the disciplines of that Order, and the task that faced him was in essence not unlike that which had faced St Dominic. It was, after all, to protect the faith, the purpose for which the Order had been founded; Pope Pius V was a worthy successor who fulfilled all the hopes of its founder. In the words of one commentator, he was one of those rare Christians who take all the words and examples of Christ literally, without exception or reservation, and so move through the world like a light in a dark place.

His government as Pope was firm as events demanded, for he was surrounded by vacillating rulers stumbling in confusion as they tried to balance compromise and concession. Despite his great age on becoming Pope, the Florentine Ambassador reported that he was 'flourishing like a rose', and so diplomatic is the remark that one is left wondering whether or not the Pope was a thorn in his side. He was quite tireless in his efforts to rally the Christian princes, and was driven to remark bitterly that they were responsible for the dire plight in which Europe found itself.

For one who normally dwelt on loftier spiritual plains, he was practical enough to point bluntly to the fate that awaited all those defeated in battle by the Turks. For at a time when unity might have given a glimmer of hope to their cause, they were busily occupied bickering amongst themselves. Both Germany and France were making conciliatory noises to Constantinople, even hoping for a share in the Islamic spoils in the seemingly inevitable event of Turkish victory. England was out of the reckoning since the Reformation which led eventually to the excommunication of Elizabeth I, placing her firmly on the fence if not on the other side.

Chesterton in his epic poem on Lepanto expresses the plight of the Pope more succinctly:

> And the Pope has cast his arms abroad for agony and loss,
> And called the kings of Christendom for swords about the
> Cross,
> The cold queen of England is looking in the glass;
> The shadow of the Valois is yawning at the Mass;
> From evening isles fantastical rings faint the Spanish gun,
> And the Lord upon the Golden Horn is laughing in the
> sun.

The only two nations remotely receptive to his plan to form a Holy League against the Infidel were themselves deeply suspicious of each other.

The first of these was the state of Venice which lay at the other end of the Mediterranean on the Adriatic Sea, her pink and white palaces reflected in the blue lagoon that separates the Serenissima from her immediate neighbours, her empire and government the envy of the world. But behind the scenes, after nearly three hundred years of costly and largely ineffective defence against the Turk, the courage of her rulers was at a low ebb. The Venetians were not helped by their own strange inability to strike a balance between spiritual matters and the more mundane subject of political gain.

When Pope Urban urged the cause of the Crusades on

them in 1203 they responded in a manner which illustrated only too vividly this conflict of interest which was to haunt them for centuries, for they never completed the arduous journey to the Holy Land. Constantinople, the treasure house of the civilized world at that time, lay in their path and proved too tempting to pass by. All thoughts of crusading were banished as they fell upon the city, sacking and looting all before them, and with their galleons almost sinking under the weight of priceless booty, they lumbered back to Venice. Perhaps the origin of the expression 'turning a blind eye' comes from this enterprise, for their aged leader, Dandolo, was sightless and could justly claim to have seen nothing. This assault left Constantinople so weakened that when the Turks finally attacked in 1453 it fell with scarcely a struggle, and the Turkish Empire, unwittingly aided by Venice, embarked upon a wave of expansion that was to last two hundred years.

By the middle of the sixteenth century, the threat to Venice itself was such that fear was no longer concealed behind gilded doors. In the last two hundred years they had witnessed the loss of all their possessions in the Aegean, and even their few outposts on the Adriatic coast were but pockets in occupied lands. The waters around the Peloponnese where centuries earlier the fleets of Anthony and Cleopatra had sailed, ceased to hold any charm for Venetian galleons. While at Navcos, inland from the bay of Lepanto, there lay the largest and southern-most dockyard of the Islamic fleet.

While the Venetians spluttered with indignation, the evidence of their eyes did little to encourage them to take a bold stand or indeed a stand of any kind. Instead they drew up their chairs and proceeded to sign as many 'peace' treaties as they could decently allow, and as one Sultan succeeded another, the Venetians expressed the uneasy hope of renewed 'relations'. Unfortunately the 'relations' envisaged by the Turk were of a different nature.

Having already crossed the Balkans and reached the gates

of Vienna, the Turks were the undisputed masters of the Arab world and they saw little reason why their advance should stop short of Europe itself.

Mehmet II, the grandfather of Suleiman the Magnificent, had vowed that he would stable his horses beneath the Dome of St Peter's and wind the Pope's head in a turban. His grandson intended to fulfil his dream.

To the Venetians, already shocked into submission by all that had gone before, there came news in 1569 that an Islamic force had landed on their treasured island of Cyprus. With uncustomary bravado a fleet was dispatched, but it merely skulked around the Mediterranean to return without honour, having failed to engage the enemy even once.

The Doges of Venice were better served by their military leader in Famagusta, for he defended the beleaguered town for eleven months against a force of 200,000 Turks. Bragadin had by his side 8,000 Christians who eventually, through exhaustion and starvation, were compelled to raise the white flag in surrender. Duped by promises of free passage, they laid down their arms and left the city, only to suffer instant death at the hands of the Turks. A worse fate awaited their leader for he was taken to a column in the city square and, before the public gaze, slowly skinned alive. The triumphant Turkish Admiral Mustapha sailed away with the stuffed skin of Bragadin hanging from the yardarm of his ship. It is hardly surprising that the Venetians were in an outraged but receptive mood when Pope Pius appealed to them to sign the League Treaty in 1570.

In Spain the situation could hardly have been more different. In Philip II the country had a ruler of rare qualities, and yet he has frequently been described as proud and devious for it has suited some historians to see him through a glass very darkly indeed.

Proud he was, but not in the accepted sense of superiority or personal haughtiness. He believed passionately in the

Divine Right of Kings and was always deeply aware of the reverence due to that station; he saw himself as the defender and champion of Catholic Europe. When he was a child, his father, Charles V, had implanted in his conscience the importance of the monarchy in protecting the people from the dangers that stalked the sixteenth century.

As if to underline the complex tasks that lay ahead and the often incomprehensible contrariness of fate, he was born at the moment when his father, the Holy Roman Emperor, and an indefatigable defender of the Catholic Church, was laying waste to the Eternal City.

When only sixteen, due to his father's continual absence abroad, Philip was made Regent of Spain, and on his father's abdication in 1555, at the age of 29 he found himself King of one of the largest empires the world had ever seen: King of Spain, of the Netherlands, of England (for he was by now married to Mary Tudor), master of Italy, Lord of such parts of the western hemisphere as had been explored, and of the Philippines so named in his honour, and above all, the right arm of the Church.

Even at that age, he so clearly perceived that Christ dwelt in the one holy Apostolic Church of Rome that he was prepared to stake treasures and kingdoms, as well as his own peace of mind and health of body, on that fact. This was the motive force which lay behind so many of the struggles in the Netherlands and France, and the reason why on numerous occasions when victory was his, he appeared to recoil from pressing the advantage or claiming valuable spoils, to the frustration of his generals and the profound disbelief of his opponents. For his quest was to free people to follow the faith, and having achieved that objective, he returned home.

One of his council described him as 'grave, serene and agreeable' and he was devoted to his family. There is a touching account of him reciting the rosary each day with his children when he was not on his travels, and on his death he bequeathed to his son a rosary of gold beads encrusted with nine rubies each, the cross with ten rubies.

His only failing was that perhaps sometimes he overestimated his personal importance in the eyes of God, for if he believed his cause to be just he was prepared to take arms against the Pope, and indeed with a great sense of self-righteousness he once dispatched his own troops, as his father had done before him, to march upon the Vatican. He frequently harboured a sense of injustice in the face of papal disapproval for he felt, with some cause, that he drove himself to the point of bankruptcy in the defence of the Church.

It was on just such an occasion that the Pope turned to him with the request that he should once more muster his forces for the defence of Christendom.

The Turkish problem was nothing new to Spain. In the seventh century the Muslims from North Africa had invaded Spain, and only after the Crusades did the Spanish knights rise to reconquer their own lands, finally succeeding during the reign of Philip's great-grandparents, Isabel and Ferdinand.

However, in history nothing is ever so neatly cut and dried, and the problem remained throughout successive centuries like an open and festering wound in the body of Spain. The indigenous population of Moriscos, as the Muslims became known, made their presence uncomfortably felt from time to time, and in 1558 the Turkish fleets sailed up and down the Italian coast, inflicting unspeakable atrocities both there and on Sicily and Naples which were also Spanish possessions. Philip's fleet put to sea but beset by illness and finally panic on sighting the huge Turkish fleet, they were soundly defeated.

In spite of this reversal Philip was not entirely wholehearted in his response to the papal request to form a Holy League against the Turk. His treasury was at an all time low, and this led the King to reply with a caution which was widely misunderstood. He felt bound to hedge his agreement with counter-demands for financial help and concessions, which appeared niggardly in the light of what was to follow and for one who could justly claim on his death bed to have spent a life in the service of the Church.

For the newly acceded Sultan of the Turks, Selim the Sot, self-styled 'Owner of all men's necks', it seemed that the time was ripe to fulfil his dream of snatching Europe. He was encouraged by the knowledge that Philip was almost totally isolated amongst the Christian princes of Europe, and not only did he have a rebellion on his hands in the south, but his armies were fully committed at the other end of Europe. The Sultan cherished the plan of turning the Mediterranean into a Turkish lake, from whence to proceed to Spain where his informers told him the Moriscos eagerly awaited his arrival.

Yet even as Philip pondered within the cold corridors of his unfinished palace of the Escorial, the Venetians' courage was ebbing. While arguing over the price of building ships, they were furtively considering a last-minute deal with the Turks to avoid the awesome prospect of Ali Pasha at the head of his immense fleet.

None of these political conundrums and diplomatic manoeuvres were of the remotest interest to Pope Pius V. In long periods of silent prayer he contemplated only the principles behind all human behaviour, unclouded by triviality of any sort, and was able to see with complete clarity the situation as it really was. He was a true Dominican, with the defence of the faith as his primary task amidst an awareness of the dangers which threatened to overwhelm Europe should it fall to Islam in the wake of North Africa and the Eastern Empire.

Beyond the conflicting political interests of Venice and Spain, Pius V had always represented the wider spiritual concept of a European alliance against the Turkish aggressors, and he signed his name to the league agreement on 7 March, 1571, the feast day of St Dominic. With tears in his eyes he placed the Christian cause in the hands of Our Lady, from whom the Spanish saint had received the rosary.

The devotion of Pius V to the Blessed Virgin had begun in childhood and her prayer of the rosary was specially dear to him, for the power of prayer over all human vanity was for this man proved beyond doubt. Only two years earlier in a Papal Bull he had instructed the faithful in the prayer of the rosary as the most powerful weapon against error. After he became Pope he was a familiar sight in the streets of Rome walking amongst the people clad still in the simple robes of a Dominican monk, deep in the prayer of the rosary and oblivious of all around him.

Despite all the political manoeuvring, he remained calmly aware of the real nature of the conflict and of the gravity of the threat which faced the Church. Of that he had no doubt. The only matter that ruffled the papal demeanour was the disarray amongst those who should have been unanimous in their support. The fact that his treasury reserves were at an all time low and in no state to finance the rebuilding of the papal fleet was of secondary importance. His great generosity not only to the poor of Rome, but to the beleaguered English Catholics in exile, and his endless ransom payments to the Turks for the release of Christian slaves, had almost emptied the papal coffers.

Not the least achievement of this remarkable Pope was the welding together of two such disparate personalities, on the one hand the velvet piety of the Spanish and on the other the gilded duplicity of the Venetians, and yet these were united in the great fighting force that confronted Ali Pasha on 7 October, 1571. For if ever proof of the power of prayer was needed, regardless of subsequent astonishing events, this surely was it. The sanctity of the Pope and his apparent aloofness from strife must have dumbfounded the practised diplomats of Madrid and Venice, and after two months of haggling they duly signed the League Treaty.

Philip not only agreed to send his half-brother, Don John of

Austria, to command the fleet but made a huge contribution in terms of ships and troops at a time when he was heavily committed elsewhere. In the event Spain undertook to provide half the total cost of the force, with Venice supplying two-thirds of the remainder. The Pope and the Knights of Malta were left to find the final third. So amply were the prayers of the Pope answered that not only did the Venetians rebuild the small fleet of the Holy See, but in the battle that followed their Admiral placed himself and his fleets under the command of Don John, an undreamt of act of humility for a Venetian.

Amidst the mêlée of mounting excitement as preparations took place on both sides, there was only one figure who remained lost in silent thought, Selim the Sot, 'Lord of all the Earth', gazing across the Adriatic was heard to say softly that more than any galleys the Holy League could set against him, he feared the prayers of Pius V.

The power of the papal prayer must have been renowned indeed for the Sultan uttered these words in the full knowledge that his own fleet was vastly superior to that of the Holy League. He could also take comfort in the knowledge that the legendary might of his fighting men was a daunting prospect for the strange and motley assortment that found themselves despatched from different parts of Europe to sail under the banner of the Holy League. Even the Knights of Malta can have had little heart for renewed battle, despite the rhetoric proclaiming the contrary which flowed from their drastically reduced numbers.

In July 1571 Don John finally set out from Madrid for Naples where he met Cardinal Granville to receive the banner of the Holy League, and from there he proceeded to Messina to take command of the fleet that was assembling there. During those last weeks of July the allied squadrons gathered for their final councils of war and it was while the Venetian fleet was sailing to join them that the Sultan finally defeated the brave Bragadin in Cyprus.

Meanwhile when news reached Spain that the grand fleet of the Turk had set sail from Constantinople, Philip had travelled to the shrine of Our Lady of Guadalupe. All the events of the last few months culminated in this moment when the talking ceased and the reality of the battle ahead dawned on all those taking part.

To those who were apprehensive, the Pope commended the protection of Our Lady, and the rosary was recited daily in every ship for the ensuing weeks. As the fleets gathered, Dominicans and Jesuits passed from deck to deck hearing confessions and offering mass, while in Rome Pius V ordered prayers to be said in all convents and monasteries of the city. After days of prayer and fasting the fleet finally received orders to set sail.

The sight of the great armada sailing from the harbour was an unforgettable one for the people of Messina to recount to their children and grandchildren. As each great galley jostled for position, the shouts of the galley masters and the cheers of the men mingled in the air with the cries of wheeling gulls and the screech of canvas unfurling in the azure sky. The noise almost drowned the murmur of prayer, as on every deck friars celebrated mass, their vestments moving in the breeze.

As each ship reached the harbour mouth, the men knelt to receive the blessing of the scarlet-clad Papal Nuncio. Don John, his golden armour gleaming in the autumn sun, led the fleet from his flagship the *Real*, which sailed under the blue banner of Our Lady of Guadaloupe. As they rounded the corner and headed away from the mainland, news reached them that the enemy had been sighted in the Gulf of Lepanto, and they headed across the open sea to the straits of Ottranto.

Sailing down the Greek coastline, they saw signs of recent Turkish raids on the island of Corfu. The desecrated churches and the mutilated bodies of their victims bore witness to frenzied enemy attacks, urging the Christian League to press on for they knew now that the enemy could not be far away.

On the evening of 6 October, Pius V led the prayer of the rosary at his own Dominican convent of Minerva in Rome, and on the morning of 7 October, 1571, as the fog that had prevailed for several days dispersed, the fleet of the Holy League rounded the headland in full sight of the gulf of Lepanto and the enemy fleet.

In the moments that followed their arrival, the shouts and the clattering of swords and scimitars died away and there was an eerie silence as nearly 100,000 men prepared for battle.

Don John arranged his armada in three lines, the Venetians under their Admiral Venier on the left, the Genoese on the right, and the young Admiral himself at the head of the papal fleet in the centre. The huge Turkish fleet sailed out of Navkapos Harbour in traditional Islamic crescent formation until on sighting the size of the Holy League force, they straightened into line abreast.

In the early morning light the crimson pennant emblazoned in gold with the words of the prophet billowed over the flagship *Sultana*, sailing under its anonymous Islamic Admiral Ali Pasha, who carried as his macabre mascot the tooth of Muhammad encased in a crystal ball. In the last moments before battle commenced, Don John boarded the fastest of his brigantines and sailed along the lines of Christian ships, inspecting his fleet and holding aloft a great iron cross. Returning to his flagship in silence, he unfurled a dazzling banner of blue damask with the figure of Christ crucified embroidered in gold thread surmounting the allied emblems.

The air was rent with tumultuous cheering from every Christian ship, almost drowning the shouting and jeering from the Turks, as the lines of galleys surged forwards.

The two flagships converged on each other at great speed, and amidst the crashing and splintering of wood, they became locked in each other's rigging thus creating a solid platform for the proceeding battle. For two hours wave upon wave of janissaries appeared from reserve ships to reinforce the hand-to-hand fighting.

Further to the left, the Turks tried to outflank the Venetian galleys by slipping through the narrows close to the coast, but this manoeuvre was thwarted and the Venetians drove them aground.

Meanwhile the Knights of Malta came under heavy attack from the Turks with a score to settle after the Great Siege of Malta, and the Knights fought with their customary courage but the numbers against them were overwhelming. In the mêlée, the Knights lost their flagship and with it the banner of St John.

After sailing up and down the lines of his fleet, Don John placed himself in the vanguard where he could confront Ali Pasha in person. The Turkish Admiral was almost immediately felled by a cannon ball which instantly beheaded him. This was the turning point in the battle and by sunset the Turkish fleet was in total disarray.

The casualties were heavy: 7,500 Christian lives had been lost and twelve galleys sunk. Of the Turkish armada, all but forty-five of their ships had foundered. 30,000 men had perished and 15,000 Christian galley slaves were freed.

During the early evening on the day of the battle Pope Pius was in the midst of discussions in his small study in the Vatican when he suddenly broke away from his companions and crossed to the window. He paused, and with a radiant smile turned to announce that a great victory had been won that day for the Holy League. This was more than two weeks before the official courier from Venice arrived in Rome. The victory of Lepanto exploded the myth of Turkish domination at sea, Ottoman sea power was contained for the foreseeable future in the eastern Mediterranean and Europe breathed a sigh of relief.

In Rome Pius V, giving joyful thanks for the deliverance of Christian Europe, decreed that 7 October would thereafter be the feast of Our Lady of Victories.

For the Knights of Malta, the victory of Lepanto had an ironic significance. So complete was their triumph over Islamic sea power, that never again was there need for the monks of war to sail out beneath the Christian banner, and the Order gradually reverted to its original role of nursing.

The praises lavished on Don John by the allies, and above all by the Pope, were not wholeheartedly endorsed by Philip, who strangely denied his young Admiral a hero's welcome in Madrid. However, nothing can alter the fact that history acclaims this 24-year-old Spanish prince for the execution of one of the finest victories at sea.

The pennant of the Turkish Admiral, Ali Pasha, was triumphantly carried to Spain where Philip caused it to be hung on the walls of the Escorial. Prayers of thanksgiving were offered throughout Spain, and Philip decreed that after his death his coffin should be lined with timbers from the Spanish galleons that had fought at Lepanto.

The Venetians were loud in their rejoicing and great was their pride when the galley *Angelo Gabriele* sailed into the lagoon trailing a Turkish flag and rows of turbans from its stern, and to this day the pennant holds pride of place on the ceiling of the Doge's palace. Slightly faded over the years from its original scarlet, the golden inscription upon it is frayed from both the passage of time and the strains of battle.

The Venetians took great pride in the bravery of their sailors, who had given their lives in greater numbers than any other ally, and their Admiral Sebastian Venier eventually succeeded as Doge of Venice.

In thanksgiving for such miraculous deliverance after three hundred years of continuous marauding by the Turkish fleet, the Venetians commissioned the building of a chapel to Our Lady of the Rosary. The walls were lined with records of the battle for there was no doubt in the Venetian mind of the cause of their victory, and having proclaimed this debt, they inscribed the legend for all to see: *Non virtus, non arma, non*

94

duces sed Mariae Rosiae victores nos fecit - neither valour, nor arms, nor leaders but Our Lady of the Rosary gave Victory.

Pius V lived just long enough to witness the great victory of Lepanto and died six months later. His successor, Pope Gregory XIII, in 1573 granted the Feast of Our Lady of Victories to all churches with an altar of the rosary, and as if to prove the extreme caution of the Church in these matters, a century and a half passed before the feast was granted to the Universal Church.

With the Turkish threat at sea now a thing of the past it was nearly a century before the dread of Muslim invasion in Europe was banished. While the events of the Reformation continued to divide and occupy most of Europe, the Turks lost no opportunity to snap at the edges of the Empire until gradually the new-found power of the Habsburgs breathed life into the ailing alliance, and the Christian forces gained the strength to gather themselves once more.

During a campaign that produced great deeds of courage in the face of vastly superior forces which was reminiscent of the siege of Malta so many years before, the beleaguered city of Vienna held out for six weeks in the summer of 1663. But the Turks had become sated with luxury and the picture they presented was quite different to the well ordered crescent of galleys that sailed into Christian view in 1571.

On this occasion they lumbered towards Vienna, a vast procession of 200,000 men led by Kara Mustapha, whose Sultan vastly preferred hunting in the forests of the Danube and whose 800 falcons wore collars and hoods encrusted with diamonds and pearls. But his Grand Vizier Mustapha was more businesslike and he settled his troops in 25,000 tents which formed a great circle around Vienna, and they prepared for a siege of limitless duration. However, the courage and faith of the Poles came to their rescue after a stirring and urgent appeal from Pope Innocent XI.

On 3 September, the incarcerated citizens of Vienna saw

flares in the sky which heralded their rescue, and under John Sobieska, the Polish horsemen came galloping down the hills to the north of the city, completely overpowering the Turkish army who were in rout by nightfall, leaving a strangely littered battlefield behind them.

The final victory over the Ottoman hordes came in 1716 when Prince Eugene defeated the remnants of the Islamic forces at Peterwarden, and it was then that Pope Clement XI commanded that the Feast of the Most Holy Rosary be celebrated by the Universal Church.

CHAPTER SIX

My sister, my bride is a garden enclosed,
the fountain sealed.

Song of Songs

In 1987 an American of half Lebanese extraction who was a journalist and author by profession, was kidnapped in southern Beirut. It was a personal crisis played out against the backdrop of war torn Lebanon, where tragedy and violence are the inheritance of the final breakup of the Ottoman Empire.

Since 1919 the Lebanon and its neighbours had become the battlefield for warring factions of Islamic tribes, (both Catholic and Orthodox) and Jewish settlers, all of whom were gradually destroying their once beautiful homeland.

In the familiar pattern of kidnapping, whoever the protagonist may be and in whatever form his demands are brazenly imposed on a bewildered world, there is above all the tragedy of the luckless victim. He becomes a mere pawn in the game between participants, who are all too often crazed and frightened gunmen whose motives are lost in a frenzy of aggression. On this occasion, their motives were well known and rational – it was to put pressure on the United States and to force Washington to sell weapons to Iran.

The kidnapping was carried out by young militiamen brandishing guns at the journalist as he travelled through the city accompanied by his Muslim friend and driver.[1] He was taken, blindfolded and handcuffed, and finally separated from his companions, left in solitary confinement. Initially he was held under the nervous supervision of guards whom he recognized merely by the shape of their feet, which was all that he could see beneath his blindfold.

After four weeks he was moved to another part of the city. His guards were now more efficient, and lengthy interrogations were interspersed with days of darkness, shackled to his bed by his feet, his hands tied and his eyes covered.

He thought of his family, in his mind he wrote the novel he had been planning, and he prayed. By drawing threads from his blindfold he gathered sufficient cotton to knot into a rosary.

After an altercation with his guards, the few possessions he had retained were removed, and amongst them his rosary. He started again, this time drawing threads from his bug-ridden blanket, and made another rosary. After sixty-three days in captivity, he escaped.

It was the only successful escape undertaken by a Western hostage from that violent city and although, as he modestly stated afterwards, it was neither particularly heroic nor courageous, it was miraculous.

Whilst his guards slept only inches from him, he had managed to free himself from his fetters and slip silently from the room that had been his prison. He was fully aware that the slightest noise could draw the inevitable consequence of a violent death, and yet he felt the certain presence of God and an extraordinary certainty that all would be well. He even felt the insistence of the Blessed Virgin that he should wear sandals – an instruction he chose to ignore or at least argue with, on the grounds that to wear shoes would impede his agility in climbing over the roof tops. In the event, no climbing was called for, and as he fled down the deserted streets of Beirut, he realized that he should have listened to that insistent voice, for his feet were cut and bleeding as he ran through the broken glass that littered his path.[2]

Three years earlier, and some sixteen hundred miles to the north-west, another faltering empire was given its notice.

A picture was flashed across the world's media of a portentous meeting in Poland. At first glance it seemed to present a familiar enough scene of men facing each other across a table, and yet it was profoundly different. On one side of the table sat a group of heavy-set and powerful men, and on the other stood a rather small and shabby man, flanked by two others. The message of intimidation was clear.

The picture was followed by an account of the meeting held between the Communist rulers of Warsaw and a troublesome Trade Union leader who was apparently threatening the unthinkable, a strike of the workers of the Gdansk shipyard. His name was Lech Walesa, and in his hand, unseen by his adversaries but visible to the camera, he held a small wooden rosary.

The picture was perhaps the first public evidence of the impending collapse of Communism and of the totalitarianism that had gripped the people of Eastern Europe for nearly seventy years. In 1917 atheistic Communism had been launched on the world, whilst Europe still reeled from the onslaught of the first World War.

Twenty-seven days after the outbreak of that Revolution, Mary appeared to three small children and laid down the only conditions for peace in the world and for staving off the punishment of God.

The timing of the apparition was crucial, and it took place in Fatima, a small village in the mountains of Portugal, the land which with Spain, forms part of the Iberian peninsula, the birthplace of St Dominic and the land from which Don John of Austria sailed forth to Lepanto.

When asked by the three children who she was, Mary replied 'I am the Lady of the Rosary' and instructed them to follow her in prayer. Francis, the only child of the three who was unable to see her, was told to take up his beads and pray. As soon as he did so his eyes were opened and he too could see the 'beautiful lady'.

Our Lady requested the children to return on the thirteenth day of each month, and on 13 July, 1917 she spoke these words:

'I shall ask for the consecration of Russia to my Immaculate Heart, as well as communion of reparation on the first Saturday of the month. If my requests are granted Russia will be converted and there will be peace. Otherwise Russia will spread her errors through the world, raising up wars and persecutions against the Church. Many will be martyred, the Holy Father will have much to suffer, several nations will be wiped out. The outlook is therefore gloomy. But my Immaculate Heart will finally triumph; the Holy Father will consecrate Russia to me; she will be converted and an era of peace will be conceded to the world. In Portugal the faith will always be preserved.'

It is interesting that Mary did not appear to those in power, to politicians or leaders of this world. Had she done so, it might have avoided all the confusion and disbelief encountered by those who were given such world-shattering messages.

In most instances the children did not even understand the message themselves and they had to repeat the Lady's words, in order carefully to relay them later and then to face the inevitable scepticism that followed. The Blessed Virgin was not drawn to the worldly or sophisticated of this world, but to innocence. The children were not even particularly saintly. They obediently said their prayers, and would rush through them, only saying the first words of each prayer so that they could return to their games, but in their innocence they knew no better.

Mary is not unreasonable in her demands, she knows that not all men will embrace her message, and asks only that enough people will recite her prayer, and we who always seek proof know her words to be true.

When the Soviets left Vienna in 1955 their withdrawal was complete and, with hindsight, to many inexplicable, for it was the first withdrawal from foreign territory since their period of expansion began in 1917. However, it is on record that the immense numbers committed to the Confraternity of the Rosary added their prayers to the hopes of the Austrians. The date of the Soviet withdrawal was 13 May, the anniversary of Fatima.

At the close of the Holy Year in 1951, solemn High Mass was sung in Fatima in the Russian Uniate Rite, by a Bishop who had recently escaped from a Soviet prison. 'Russia will be converted', Mary said, and in Fatima the Icon of Our Lady of Kazan has been kept for many years until such time as it is returned to its home in Russia.

How different were the children after seeing the 'beautiful Lady'. Their only wish was to be with her, to pray as she had commanded and to grieve over the sins of the world which so offend Our Lord. 'Men must amend their lives and ask pardon for their sins. Man must no longer offend Our Lord, who is already offended too much.' These words were spoken at Fatima on the day of the great miracle of the sun, a miracle promised by Our Lady to the children, who repeatedly asked her for a sign for those who doubted.

The miracle has been well documented both by press reports and accounts given by many of the thousands who witnessed the sun apparently tumbling from the sky, before spinning and casting strange beams of light across the earth. Many came out of curiosity and scepticism, like the director of the Lisbon daily paper, O *Seculo*.

However, his report of 15 October ends with the words: 'Only one thing remains now to be done, namely for the scientists to explain from the height of their learning, the fantastic dance of the sun, which today at Fatima has drawn "Hosanna" from the hearts of the faithful; and which, as trustworthy people assure me, has impressed even Free-thinkers, as well as others of no religious convictions who had come to this spot, henceforth celebrated.'

Today, an immense Basilica stands near the spot at the

103

Cova da Iria where Our Lady appeared, now constantly thronging with thousands of pilgrims who travel from all over the world, many completing the last two hundred miles on foot. Throughout the day and night the prayer of the rosary is recited in every language. And two miles beyond the Basilica, visits are made to the little village of Ajustral where the children lived.

The cobbled path which is still the country route to Ajustral winds its way through the groves of olive and pine trees and the wild thyme that grows amongst the rocks; past the Stations of the Cross, each one donated by different Hungarian parishes whose members, expelled by Communism, were scattered throughout the United States. The path continues to the 14th Station at the top of the hill, where there is a chapel dedicated to St Stephen, King of Hungary.

From there, one gazes from the little medieval village of Fatima on one side to the extraordinary testimony of the twentieth century, to the miracle of the Cova da Iria, now a mass of hotels and mother-houses of religious orders from around the world, and towering over all, the slender spire of the Basilica topped by a golden crown, its bells pealing out the song of Fatima on the hour.

The sounds amongst the olive groves are probably no different now to those of sixty years ago, the song of birds, the distant bleating of goat herds, dogs barking, and from Ajustral, the harsh voices of the women as they work in the fields. The only alien sound is the hammering of builders as they build more and more accommodation for the millions of pilgrims . . . .

Amidst this scene one comes upon the place where Mary appeared to the three children on the one occasion when they were prevented from keeping their appointment at the Cova da Iria, the same trees moving gently in the breeze and all stray thoughts fading from the mind. Peace and silence invade the air.

In that unearthly silence I pondered on the real meaning of the rosary. In recounting a story or history, it is always tempting to concentrate on the dramatic, on great events whose description bears testimony to the expressed view. In describing the deeds of St Dominic in Albi, and the great battle of Lepanto, and most recently the outcome of the words spoken at Fatima, it is satisfying to recount such world-shaking events as evidence of the power of the rosary.

But what is really under discussion is the power of prayer, and to speak of it in such worldly terms can be counter-productive. To hear the words 'Faith can move mountains' has always seemed daunting, and I turn away disconsolate in the certainty that my own faith would not move a mountain.

Above all the rosary is practical. Beginning with gardens and the simple longing for Paradise, it rested on the certainty that a knowledge of the Scriptures based on the mystery of the Incarnation is the source of Christian hope.

Whether they be made from the thread of a hostage's blindfold, a piece of wood or priceless jewels, the beads are a comforting presence, so ordinary and practical and yet they represent the most extraordinary and supernatural act imaginable, the contact between man and his Creator. The beads can be carried in a pocket or a bag and nothing could be less remarkable. We seem, for the most part, to have forgotten that the original meaning of the word bede was prayer.

To compare our life of prayer with the labour of a gardener is probably not immediately obvious. The need for patient industry, of the quiet happiness to be gained by working the soil, of planting a seed and tending the plant until such time as it is harvested – it is the source of our earthly existence.

The early Christian made the connection with prayer quite naturally and he was seeking not drama, merely the right to a life both material and spiritual.

Above all, it is simple and uncomplicated. Undoubtedly great miracles have been wrought by the prayer of the rosary but there is an even greater miracle of continuity and faith sustained through the centuries.

The search for the history of the rosary began in England, and I wanted finally to return to one of the greatest shrines in Europe, forgotten for many centuries but now restored. Miracles have taken place there, it is even rumoured that the sun has danced while people recited the rosary but we do not need to rely on these great events to understand Walsingham and the shrine of Our Lady.

The approach to the village gives no hint of what lies ahead as roads peter into lanes in the gentle Norfolk countryside, and one's thoughts turn with concern to the pilgrims on foot who must leap aside as the farm tractors drive past.

Today there is an air of peace and silence in Walsingham which to the English temperament makes it a place of wonder and holiness. It settles securely into the rolling countryside, unostentatious and serene. I have always been here, it seems to say, I am part of England's history and the focus of the dowry of Mary.

The Slipper Chapel, so named for it was here that the pilgrims removed their shoes to travel the last part of the journey bare-footed, settles into the hedgerow surrounded by wild flowers on one side, as if leaning away, in dismay, from the 'pilgrim centre' that has been built by its side. The statue of Our Lady of Walsingham rests in this chapel on the edge of the village of Walsingham where once the shrine, now a ghostly ruin, was the wonder of Europe.

Until the Reformation, the journeying of pilgrims to Mary's shrine was continuous and the list is lengthy of Kings and Queens who came to pray to Our Lady and to bring gifts in gratitude for favours received. The precise record of their gifts, of money to pay for the King's candle, for the priests singing before the statue of the Virgin, add to the picture of the prosperity of Walsingham as a flourishing pilgrim centre, and together with the numerous inns, they make up an image of great festivity and mutual well-being.

All this came abruptly to an end in 1534 when the Canons of the Priory agreed, with hardly a demur, to the Act of the King's Supremacy. The shrine was destroyed and the statue of the Virgin taken to Chelsea in London, and destroyed.

There followed the ruthless martyrdom of the pathetic few who voiced regret at the desecration of their shrine, and they were quickly dealt with by Cromwell's authority. There were the brave recusant families who kept vigil for Our Lady over the ensuing centuries, and a testimony to the pain of such a bitter loss was left by Philip, Earl of Arundel:

Owls do shriek where the sweetest hymns
Lately were sung;
Toads and serpents hold their dens
Where the palmers did throng.
Weep, weep, O Walsingham,
Whose days are nights,
Blessings turned to blasphemies,
Holy deeds to despites.
Sin is where Our Lady sat,
Heaven turned is to hell.
Satan sits where Our Lord did sway;
Walsingham, O, farewell.[3]

The silence continued undisturbed until the end of the nineteenth century, when a devout Christian named Charlotte Boyd acquired the Slipper Chapel, restored it, and entrusted it to the care of the Abbot of Downside. Within a year of Miss Boyd's arrival, the first official pilgrimage since the Reformation took place and since then they have become a regular occurrence.

When Pope John Paul II visited England in 1982, the statue of Our Lady of Walsingham was taken to rest on the altar in Wembley Stadium where he celebrated mass before a crowd of more than a hundred thousand people. The statue was then returned to the Slipper Chapel on the outskirts of Walsingham.

The lane from the Slipper Chapel is named the Milky Way, after the relic known as 'Our Lady's Milk', from a rock in Bethlehem which turned white after Mary had visited it. It leads between hedges so tall that they seem to blinker one's view from any diversion, so that all thoughts are on Walsingham which lies ahead.

Some of the inns in the village still flourish and there are shops selling statues and rosaries, but so discreetly that one is aware of the difference between the cheerful commercialism that sits happily around continental shrines, and this almost refined reserve.

The site of the ruined shrine that was once the equal of Ely Cathedral is now privately owned. On paying an entrance fee, one is led down a path and into what appears at first to be a leafy private garden, and the atmosphere is at once hallowed and still. The birds remind one of St Francis who would have immediately recognized their song as a continuous praise of God.

There were a few people wandering through the garden in the afternoon sun peering at the stones that mark out the perimeter of buildings long since gone.

I thought of the scene that would have confronted the visitor before the dissolution of the monasteries, of the litanies and hymns that were sung by the thousands of pilgrims who came to Our Lady, their advocate, with their prayers and hopes, certain that she would place them before her Son. It all seemed rather forlorn.

As I stood lost in thought, a sound caused me to turn and behind me I saw the stream running beneath a small bridge that lay ahead. The discovery filled me with happiness for I had forgotten that water is always present at the shrines of Mary. At Fatima and Lourdes it sprang from the ground at her command, but at Walsingham it had been slightly different.

In 1061 when a young widow named Richelda had a dream in which Mary showed her the Holy House of Nazareth, she immediately planned to build such a house at Walsingham. The exact siting of the chapel proved unaccountably difficult and Richelda, the record tells us, turned in prayer to the angels, who directed her to a site beside two wells and the builder then carried out her wishes.

'My sister, my spouse, is like a garden enclosed, a fountain sealed.' It seemed as though Mary had always been there, waiting patiently for our return with our endless requests and prayers.

The 'Garden enclosed' was the medieval symbol of the Incarnation upon which Christianity is based, that gives so true an understanding of the world. Of a world that is the marriage of matter and spirit, the divine and the human, for whom the prayer of the rosary involving both mind and body is so perfectly suited.

✛

Notes

Chapter 1

1. Genesis 2:8
2. Isaiah 58:11
3. Song of Solomon 4:12
4. Eleanor Sinclair Rhode, *Garden Craft in the Bible*, London 1927
5. Butler's *Lives of the Saints*, London & Dublin 1954
6. Julia Berrell, *The Garden*, Thames & Hudson 1966, p. 92.
7. Theresa McLean, *Mediaeval Gardens*, Collins 1981

Chapter 2

1. Father Bidgett, *Our Lady's Dowry*, London, Burns & Oates, p. 102.
2. Watterton, *Pietas Mariana Britannica*, St Joseph's Catholic Library London 1879, p. 43.
3. Migne Patrilogia, *Sermon 20*, Tom; cvcv col. 522–24
4. Maisie Ward, *The Splendour of the Rosary*, Sheed & Ward 1946, p. 42
5. *The Nun's Rule being the Ancren Riwle*, Alexandra Moring Ltd London 1905
6. *Speculum Ecclesiae* Cap xxii: Bib Max Tom xvv
7. *The Month* 1900
8. Luke 21:19
9. Father Thurston, *The Month*, December 1900

10. 'A *relation of the Island of England*', printed for the Camden Society

Chapter 3

1. Bede Jarrett O.P., *The Life of St Dominic*, Blackfriars Publications London 1955, p. 92

Chapter 4

1. *The Biography of Ser Marco Polo – The Venetian*, translated and edited by Col. Henry Yule, Vol. II, p. 275, John Murray 1871.
2. Father Bidgett, *Our Lady's Dowry*
3. *Testamenta Eboracensia*, Vol 14, Surtees Society 1868, p. 257
4. Sir H. Nicholas, *Testamenta Vestuta*, p. 141
5. *Testamenta Eboracensia*, Vol 1V, Surtees 1868, p. 231
6. *Testamenta Eboracensia*, Vol IV, Surtees 1868, p. 231
7. *Testamenta Eboracensia*, Vol IV, Surtees 1868, p. 27
8. Sir H. Nicholas, *Testamenta Vestuta*, p. 141
9. Joan Evans, *A History of Jewellery 1100–1870*, Faber & Faber, p. 77
10. Ibid.
11. Chaucer, The Prologue to *The Canterbury Tales*.
12. Sir Thomas More, *Dialogue of Comfort*, Ch. 14
13. Ethne Wilkins, *The Rose Garden Game*, Victor Gollancz Ltd 1969, p. 49
14. Stephen Birchington, *Life of Robert Winchelsey*

Chapter 6

1. Charles Glass, *Tribes with Flags*, Secker & Warburg London 1990
2. This story by kind permission of Charles Glass
3. E. Jones (ed), *New Oxford Book of Sixteenth-Century Verse*, 1991

✠

BIBLIOGRAPHY

Anderson, Robin, *St Pius V*, Tan Books, Illinois 1978.

Belloc, Hilaire, *The Great Heresies*, Sheed & Ward, London 1938.

Bergin, Robert, *This Apocalyptic Age*, Voice of Fatima International 1970.

Bradford, Ernle, *The Great Seige – Malta 1656*, Hodder & Stoughton 1961.

Brady, Gerard K., *St Dominic Pilgrim of Light*, Burns & Oates, London 1957.

Bridgett, Father, *Our Lady's Dowry*, Burns & Oates Ltd., London 1894.

Burrell, Julia, *The Garden*, Thames & Hudson 1966.

Butlers Lives of the Saints, Virtue & Co., Ltd., Dublin 1954.

Duffy, Eamon, *The Stripping of the Altars*, Yale University Press, New Haven and London 1993.

Evans, Joan, *A History of Jewellery 1100-1870*, Faber & Faber, London.

Gillett, H. M., *Shrines of England and Wales*, Samuel Walker Ltd. 1957.

Glass, Charles, *Tribes with Flags – A Journey Curtailed*, Secker and Warburg, London 1990.

Harty, Gabriel, *Rediscovering the Rosary*, O.P. Veritas Publications 1979.

Harvey, John, *Mediaeval Gardens*, Collins, London 1981.

Harvey, Lawrence, F., *By the Queen's Command*, Burns & Son, Glasgow, 1951.

Harvey, T. Edmund, *St Aelred of Rivaulx*, H.R. Allenson Ltd., 1932.

Jameson, Mrs, *Legends of the Madonna*, Longmans & Green, 1909.

Jarrett, Bede, *The Life of St Dominic (1170–1221)*, C. P. Blackfriars, 1955.

Knowles, David, *Monastic Order in England*, Cambridge University Press, 1940.

Johnson, John S., *The Rosary in Action*, Tan Books, 1954.

McLean, Theresa, *Mediaeval English Gardens*, Collins, London 1981.

Montfort, St Louis de, *The Secret of the Rosary*, Montfort Publications, New York 1965.

Morton, James (ed.), *The Nun's Rule being the Ancren Riwle*, Alexandra Moring Ltd., De la More Press, London 1905.

Ousler, Fulton, *The Happy Grotto*, The World's Work, Surrey 1913.

Parkinson, Francis, *Bernadette of Lourdes*, Keyes, 1953.

Pietas Mariana Britannica, Waterton St Joseph's Catholic Library, 1879.

Sinclair Rhode, Eleanor, *Garden Craft in the Bible*, Herbert Jenkins, London 1927.

Runciman, Stephen, *The Crusades*, C.U.P., 1951.

Sumption, Jonathan, *The Albigensian Crusade*, Faber & Faber, 1978.

Thurston, Father, *Series on the Rosary, Month Magazine* 1900.

Walsh, William Thomas, *Philip II*, Sheed & Ward, London 1938.

Wilkins, Eithne, *The Rose Garden*, Victor Gollancz Ltd., London 1969.